✕ ✕ Sew your style! ✕ ✕

FABRIC PAPER THREAD

26 Projects to Stitch with Friends

Kristen Sutcliffe

FunStitch STUDIO

stitch your art out.

Text copyright © 2013 by Kristen Sutcliffe

Photography and Artwork copyright © 2013 by C&T Publishing, Inc.

Publisher: Amy Marson

Creative Director: Gailen Runge

Art Director/Book Designer: Kristy Zacharias

Editor: Cynthia Bix

Technical Editors: Sandy Peterson and Gailen Runge

Cover Designer: April Mostek

Production Coordinator: Zinnia Heinzmann

Production Editor: Joanna Burgarino

Illustrator: April Mostek

Style and How-to Photography by
Christa Kimble, unless otherwise noted

Project Photography by Christina Carty-Francis and
Diane Pedersen of C&T Publishing, Inc., unless otherwise noted

Published by FunStitch Studio, an imprint of C&T Publishing, Inc., P.O. Box 1456, Lafayette, CA 94549

Library of Congress Cataloging-in-Publication Data

Sutcliffe, Kristen, 1982-

Fabric - paper - thread : 26 projects to stitch with friends / Kristen Sutcliffe.

    pages cm

ISBN 978-1-60705-715-4 (soft cover)

1. Textile crafts--Juvenile literature. 2. Paper work--Juvenile literature. I. Title.

TT712.S78 2013

745.54--dc23

2012043752

Printed in China

10 9 8 7 6 5 4 3 2 1

Dedication

For my daughter, Saya

For Grammy

Acknowledgments

First and foremost, thank you to everyone at C&T for giving me the amazing opportunity to work on this book. I have learned so much through this process. Thank you especially to Cynthia for giving me the guidance I needed to dive into work on my first book. I am in awe of your talent with words and grateful for your support and your patience.

Thank you, Sharon, for your hospitality, your friendship, your support, and all your help in getting this book done.

Thank you to Stephanie and Matt for your help.

Thank you to Madison, Madisyn, and Milana for being beautiful on the inside and out and for being so much fun to work with.

Thank you, Christa, for your beautiful photographs and for being so wonderful to work with. I'm so glad I found you!

And, of course, Junji and Saya. You are my best friends, my teammates, and my inspiration. Thank you for making sacrifices so that I could have the time and space I needed to work on this book. Thank you, Junji, for telling me that I could fail and you would still love me. I carried those words in my heart and thought of them every time I started to doubt myself. Your love and support carried me through this process. I love you both with my whole heart.

CONTENTS

HELLO, STITCHERS!

Do you love to make things? Or are you new to crafting and just want to give it a try? There is nothing I love more than making things. I can't wait to share some ideas with you! Whatever your skill level, I hope this book will inspire you to get creative—and to have fun, too.

In these pages you will find projects you can make with fabric, paper, and thread. You can make things to wear or to decorate your home. You can make something for yourself or something to give as a gift.

Many of the projects involve embroidery. I will show you how to use a needle and colorful embroidery thread to add pictures and patterns to fabric and paper. You'll also find simple sewing projects and fun, unusual ideas for using fabric and recycled materials. All the materials used in the projects are easy to find at a craft store or thrift store.

Even if you are a beginner, you will be able to make all the projects in this book. But some may take a bit more skill and patience than others. The projects are marked with one, two, or three needles. This marks their level of difficulty.

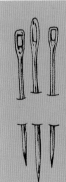

This is a simple project that you will be able to take on right away.

For this project, you'll learn a new skill.

This project may be a little tricky, or it might take a little longer, but with a little practice and patience you will be able to master it!

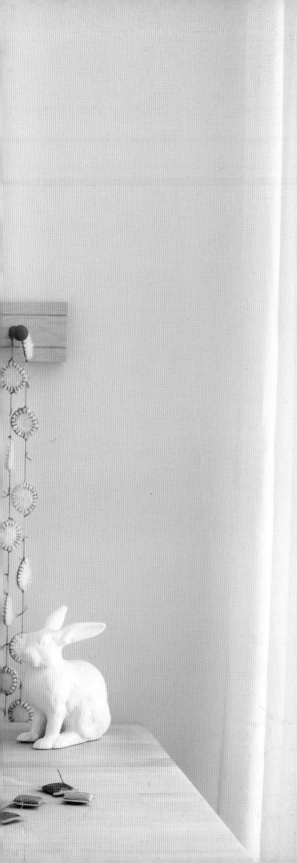

GET STARTED, GET INSPIRED

When you start crafting, you will see endless possibilities for things to make. Begin by learning some basic skills and techniques. Then you can go in any direction you choose.

To make the projects in this book, you'll need just a few simple supplies and tools.

Once you get started, you will find that certain fabrics and tools become personal favorites.

Fabrics

Hand-printed fabric: You can buy lots of wonderful print fabrics at quilt shops as well as online. I especially love hand-printed fabrics, though. They are so different and such fun! All the printed fabric shown in the projects in this book comes from Sara Lee Parker. She sells her hand-printed fabric on Etsy (etsy.com/shop/saraleeparker).

Linen: This is my favorite fabric for embroidery. For more about plain fabric to embroider on, turn to Fabric (page 21).

Leather: A couple of projects in this book call for upcycled leather. For this, you can find and cut up old purses or wallets. Used leather is soft and has a nicely worn look.

Fabrics by Sara Lee Parker

Detail of Embroidered Bracelet (page 54)

Felt & felted wool: Some projects in this book use *felt* as a backing for fabric or embroidered pieces. You can use craft felt or wool felt. Wool felt is a little more expensive, but it is great to work with. *Felted wool* is different from felt. It's made from old sweaters! In this book I'll show how you can easily wash and shrink sweaters to make soft, fuzzy felted wool.

Start with an old wool sweater.   Felted Disk Coasters (page 118)

Fusible web: One of my favorite products is Pellon 805 Wonder-Under fusible web. It's a fusible interfacing that sticks to fabric when you press it with a hot iron. You can use it to stick one fabric to another without sewing! Wonder-Under has a paper backing that comes in very handy for tracing patterns. Several projects in this book use Wonder-Under. The directions for using Wonder-Under come with the product, and I suggest you read them carefully before use. You will need an iron and ironing board to fuse it in place.

Crafting Supplies

Most of the supplies and tools you will need are pretty basic. You may already have some of them around the house. Many of the rest are easy to find at craft stores and fabric stores.

You'll need a few other simple but special items for embroidering. To find out about these, turn to Embroidery (page 20).

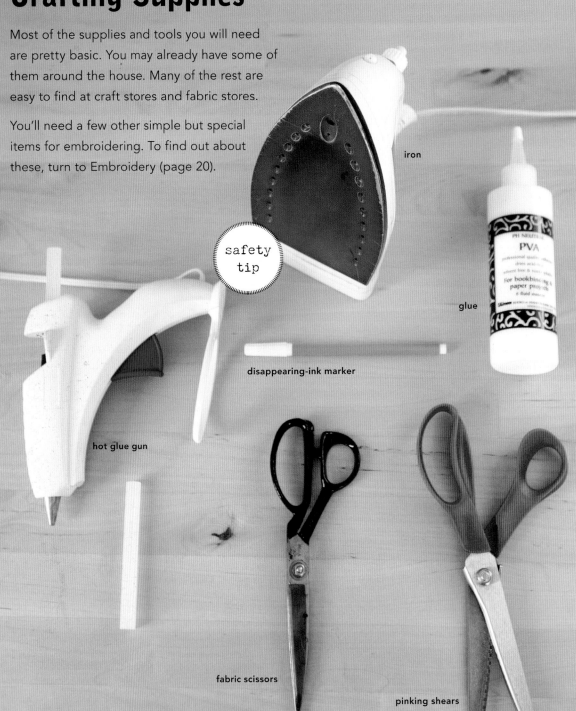

iron

safety tip

glue

disappearing-ink marker

hot glue gun

fabric scissors

pinking shears

Two tools you'll use often are an iron and a hot glue gun. An iron you know about.

A hot glue gun is a super-handy electrical tool. You load a stick of solid glue into the gun. The gun heats the glue. Then you use a trigger to squeeze out hot melted glue.

<u>Be sure to ask an adult before using these tools!</u> An iron and a hot glue gun both get very hot and can be dangerous. Keep them away from things that could catch on fire. And don't forget to unplug the cord when you are finished. Allow these tools to cool completely in a safe place before putting them away.

Do you have younger brothers or sisters? Don't use an iron or hot glue gun on the floor or where little hands can reach them!

WHAT'S CARDSTOCK?

You'll see that several projects in this book call for cardstock. Cardstock is a kind of paper that is thicker and stronger than regular printing paper but still flexible. (Think of the paper used for greeting cards or invitations.) At some art supply stores you can buy cardstock by the sheet. This is great because you can pick and choose the colors you like and buy only the amount you need. I also like to buy white and other neutral-colored cardstock by the pack so I always have some on hand.

where to shop

Where can you find the materials for the projects in this book and for all your other creative adventures? I like to look in three places.

Craft and fabric stores: Your local craft store will have tools, materials, and a decent selection of fabric. I also like to shop at local fabric stores. They often carry fabrics from independent designers or from other countries. Fabric choice is all about personal style. So take your time and look around for something that "speaks" to you.

Thrift stores: Some of the projects in this book use recycled materials. For these, head to a local thrift store. Old wool sweaters can be felted and cut up for projects. To learn about felting, read Felting a Sweater (page 96). Leather from old purses makes great bracelets.

Online: Browse online for great fabric and ribbon. Try searching for hand-printed fabrics or fun, modern Japanese fabrics. There is so much to choose from! Ask your parents to help you order some. My favorite source is Etsy (etsy.com).

Getting Inspired

You can make the projects in this book just the way they are shown. But you can also feel free to take them in your own direction. Get creative with the designs. Choose your favorite colors and fabrics to work with. That's part of the fun!

I like to start every project with a sketchbook and pen. I am not great at drawing, but that's OK. A sketchbook (without lines on the paper) is a great place to keep track of ideas as they come to you. I carry a small sketchbook in my bag wherever I go. I also have a few others at home. I love to browse shops like Anthropologie to look for beautiful empty books to fill up with notes and good ideas. Or you can get a plain book and make it your own, like the Sketchbook with Pom-Pom Bookmark (page 110).

For writing and drawing, I like to use the Marvy Uchida LePen. It has a micro-fine plastic point for drawing fine lines and comes in many colors.

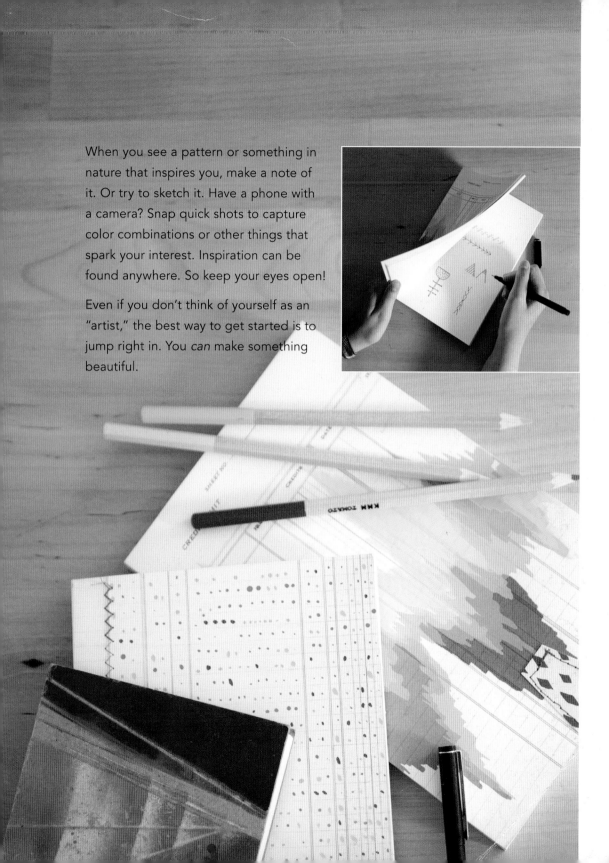

When you see a pattern or something in nature that inspires you, make a note of it. Or try to sketch it. Have a phone with a camera? Snap quick shots to capture color combinations or other things that spark your interest. Inspiration can be found anywhere. So keep your eyes open!

Even if you don't think of yourself as an "artist," the best way to get started is to jump right in. You *can* make something beautiful.

WATERCOLOR & PEN POSTCARDS

Let's start with this watercolor and pen sketching exercise. The point here is to loosen you up and get your ideas flowing. You might come up with a pattern or design that you love! Later, you could use it as an embroidery pattern for a project—like the Embroidered Bracelet (page 54) or the Stitched Paper Gift Tags (page 128).

THE MATERIALS

▷ Watercolor paper cut to postcard size (4″ × 6″)

▷ Watercolor paints and brushes

▷ Fine-point marker pen

▷ Scrap paper for practice

▷ tip

Watercolor paper is thick and textured. For this little project, inexpensive "student grade" watercolor paper, paints, and brushes from the craft store are fine. As far as pens go, use a fine-point pen.

THE STEPS

1. Get a bowl of water. Wet the paint-brush and paint. Use scrap paper to practice painting smooth, even lines. Experiment with more or less water, and with mixing colors.

2. Once you feel comfortable, paint several postcards at a time. Paint different colors of horizontal lines going across them.

3. Wait until the paint is completely dry on the postcards.

4. Use a marker pen to draw over or between the watercolor lines. Use dots and lines in different combinations to make interesting designs.

Have fun and don't worry about making it look perfect. Imperfection can be beautiful!

like this!

Gather supplies.

Paint your cards.

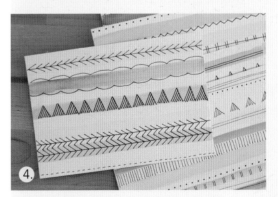

Add fine pen lines, and you're finished!

PRACTICING NEW SKILLS:
BEAUTIFUL STITCHES

Lots of the projects in this book use embroidery and hand stitching. You can use stitching to add beautiful color and pattern to the things you make. So let's learn and practice this new skill!

Embroidery

Embroidery is one of my favorite methods of getting my designs out of my head and onto fabric (or paper). I'll bet it will be the same for you! It just takes a little practice and a few simple materials.

BASIC SUPPLIES

For all the embroidery projects you will need the few basic things shown here. If you go to a craft or fabric store, you may find all these things in one section.

▷ tip

Don't feel like you have to use the same colors that I do for the projects in this book. Choose colors that speak to you!

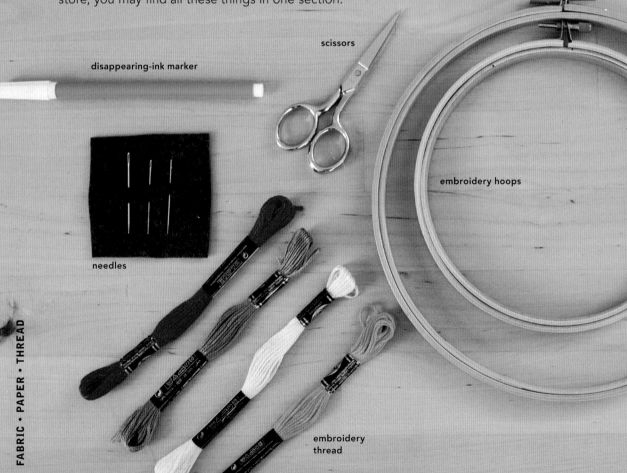

scissors

disappearing-ink marker

embroidery hoops

needles

embroidery thread

FABRIC • PAPER • THREAD

Embroidery thread (also called embroidery floss) comes in a rainbow of different colors. You can start a small collection of thread with six or eight colors, which you can combine in different ways. Later, you can add more.

Needles should be the kind marked as "embroidery needles." These needles have long eyes. They make it possible to thread multiple strands of embroidery thread. A larger needle may be easier to thread, but it will be harder to pull through tightly woven fabrics.

Embroidery hoops come in different sizes. I usually use a 5″-diameter hoop for smaller projects and a 10″ hoop for larger projects. If you are going to buy just one hoop, go for the smaller one. A smaller hoop is easier to hold and can be used with smaller pieces of fabric. If you are working on a larger project, you can always move the hoop around to different areas of the fabric as you go. Use a hoop when embroidering on linen or Aida cloth.

FABRIC

Linen is my favorite fabric for embroidery. You can embroider on almost any kind of fabric, but I recommend a fabric like linen that is woven of threads that you can see easily. Being able to see the threads makes it easier to stitch in straight lines and create geometric designs.

Aida cloth is a special fabric used for cross-stitching. You can see tiny squares in the fabric. You can fill each square with a cross-stitched x. Any pattern or image that you draw on graph paper can be easily transferred onto Aida cloth. You will see what I mean later on! Each square of the graph paper corresponds to a square on the cloth. Don't limit yourself to only cross-stitching on Aida cloth, though.

Plastic canvas is super easy to stitch on. I use this material for just one project in the book—the Cross-Stitched Backpack Label (page 132). Plastic canvas is really sturdy. It won't rip and it won't fray. You won't need to use an embroidery hoop when you stitch on it.

aida cloth

linen

plastic canvas

LET'S EMBROIDER!

With five simple stitches, you can create loads of colorful patterns. You can see these stitches in the sampler. Read on to learn how to do them.

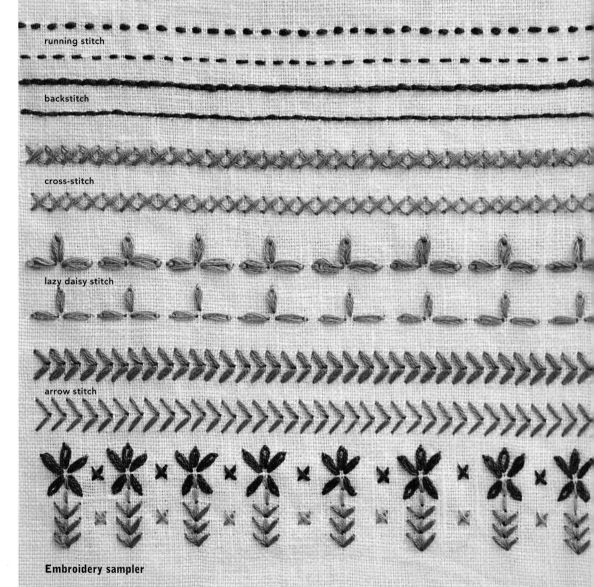

running stitch

backstitch

cross-stitch

lazy daisy stitch

arrow stitch

Embroidery sampler

SEPARATING THREAD STRANDS

Embroidery thread is made up of 6 thin strands. You can embroider with all 6 strands together or you can separate them and work with 2 or 3 strands.

Your work will have a slightly different look depending on how many strands you use. If you look at my embroidery sampler (page 22), you will see what I mean. For each type of stitch I did the first row with 6 strands and the second row with 3 strands. (The bottom row shows one way to combine several stitches to make a really special picture.)

1. To divide the strands, cut a piece of embroidery thread the length that you will need for your project. Don't make it longer than about 15˝; you don't want tangles and knots!

2. Hold the floss in one hand and carefully select the number of strands you want. *Slowly* pull them apart from the others, untwisting as you go.

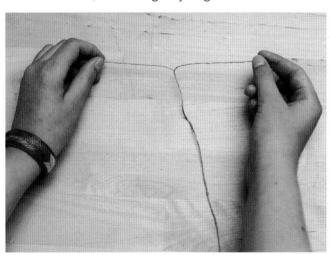

GETTING READY TO STITCH

You will need to mark your fabric with the embroidery design and put it into the hoop. Here's how.

1. Cut out a square of fabric. It should be large enough to fill the embroidery hoop with room to spare all around (even if your design is small). The project instructions in this book will tell you what size to cut. When you are finished stitching, you can cut the fabric to the smaller size that you want it to be.

2. Transfer the embroidery design onto the center of the fabric. You can trace the designs from this book. First photocopy the design. Then tape the paper to a window and put the fabric square over it. You'll be able to see the design through the fabric. Use a disappearing-ink marker to trace it. When you are finished stitching, the ink will wash away with just a little bit of water. Since the designs in this book are pretty simple, you could also draw your own design. Feel free to change it up!

3. Put your fabric into an embroidery hoop. Choose the hoop size based on the size of the project. The embroidery hoop has 2 circles. One is smaller and plain, and the other is larger and has brackets and a screw. Separate the 2 circles and loosen the screw on the larger circle. Put the fabric over the plain circle (with the finished side facing up), centering the circle as best you can. Place the other circle on top and gently press to fit it into place over the bottom one. Carefully pull the fabric edges outward to stretch the fabric taut in the hoop. Then tighten the screw to hold the fabric in place.

▷ **tip**

Be sure to read the instructions for your type of disappearing-ink marker. Remove your marks before ironing, because heat can make some marks permanent.

▷ **tip**

Another option to transfer a design from paper to fabric is by using embroidery transfer paper. You can buy transfer paper at a fabric store. Sandwich the transfer paper between the right side of the fabric and the paper with the design on it. Then trace over the design with a pen or pencil.

EMBROIDERY STITCHES

There are many kinds of embroidery stitches—some very complicated. But if you learn just the five basic stitches shown here, you can do all the projects in this book and more!

The drawings will show you how to make each type of stitch. To start, thread a needle with your chosen number of strands of embroidery thread. Tie a simple knot at the end of one set of strands.

Always start with your needle on the back or underside of the fabric and bring it through to the front side. From there, follow the numbers in the drawings. They will show the path that your needle should follow to complete the stitch.

Running stitch

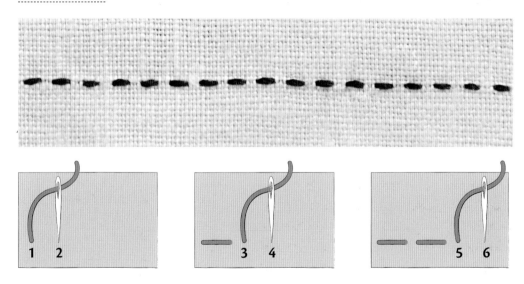

Backstitch

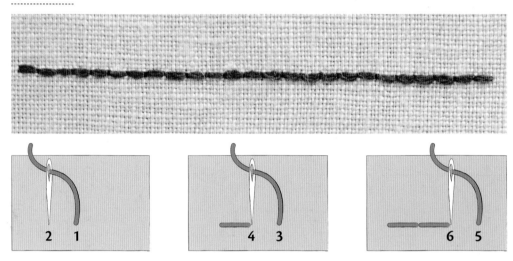

Cross-stitch

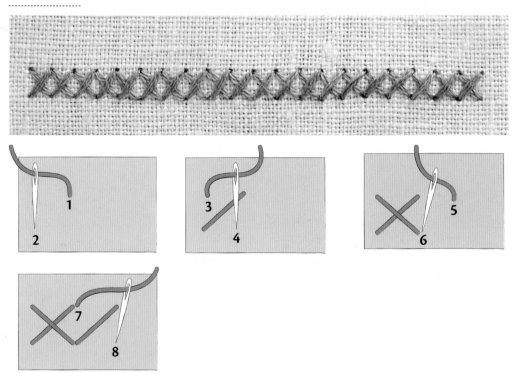

Lazy daisy stitch

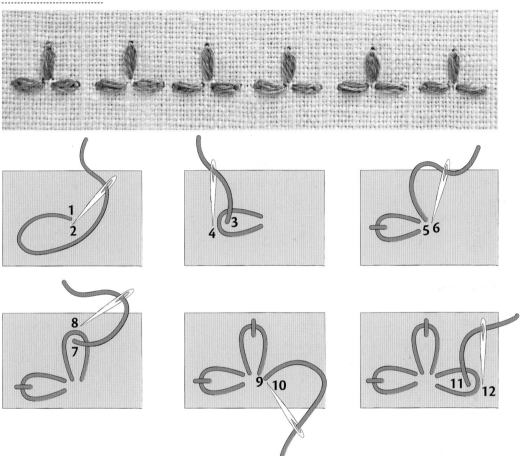

▷ tip

Lazy daisy stitches are often used to make the petals of
a flower. You can make a cute flower by doing 6 or 8 lazy
daisy stitches around a central point. Turn to the photo of
the sampler (page 22) to see how they look!

Arrow stitch

▷ tip

When you finish stitching, you need to hold the thread tails in place by running the needle under a few stitches on the back side. If you run out of thread in the middle of stitching, use this same method to end it and to start a new thread. Generally I use a knot only when I am first starting and there are no stitches yet to secure the thread tail.

Hand Sewing Stitches

There are two hand sewing stitches that will come up in this book—the whipstitch and the blanket stitch. They are different from the embroidery stitches in that they are used *around the edge* of fabrics or materials. They make a nice finishing touch to a project like the Simply Stitched Tote Bag (page 48). You can use embroidery thread for these stitches as well.

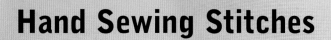

Whipstitch

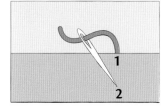
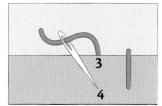
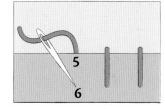

Blanket stitch

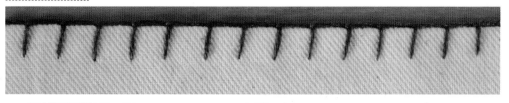

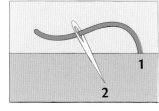
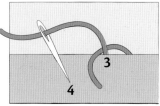
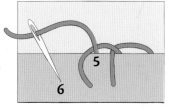

EMBROIDERY SAMPLER CARD

A sampler is a piece of fabric embroidered with examples of different stitches. Samplers are great for practicing embroidery skills. In your sampler, you can put a few different stitches together into a simple small design. Then put it to good use! With this project, you'll cut it out and use it to decorate a greeting card.

Finished card: 4″ × 6″

THE MATERIALS

▷ 4 different colors of embroidery thread

▷ Embroidery needle

▷ 5″ embroidery hoop

▷ Square of linen fabric 6″ × 6″

▷ Fabric scissors

▷ Blank card or postcard 4″ × 6″

▷ Glue

▷ Glue brush (cheap paintbrush that you don't mind ruining with glue)

THE STEPS

Embroidery pattern is on page 32. The stitches are described on pages 25–28.

1. Trace the pattern or draw your own embroidery design onto the fabric with a disappearing-ink marker. The design doesn't have to be exactly centered on the fabric because you will cut it out later. But make sure you have a generous border around all sides. Put your fabric into the embroidery hoop (page 24).

2. Cut a piece of embroidery thread no longer than 15″. Divide out 3 strands and thread your needle. Knot the thread.

3. Start stitching. The pattern tells you which stitches to make in which areas. For this design, do the top running stitches first. Follow with the lazy daisy stitches, the arrow stitches, the half-arrow stitches, and finally the running stitches again.

4. When you are finished stitching, take the fabric out of the hoop and use fabric scissors to trim away excess fabric from around the design. (Leave about a ½″ border all the way around.)

Draw design on fabric and put it in hoop. Stitch away!

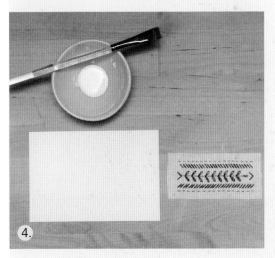

Cut out finished embroidery.

5. Spray a generous amount of water from the iron onto the fabric. This will make any ink that is left disappear. Press the fabric flat by ironing it gently, right side up. Then press again, if needed.

6. Brush the back of the embroidered fabric evenly with glue. Press and smooth it onto the center front of a blank card.

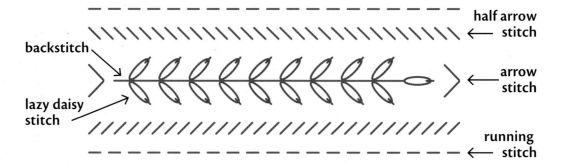

half arrow stitch

backstitch

arrow stitch

lazy daisy stitch

running stitch

like this!

6.

Glue it on your card!

EMBROIDERED PATCH 2 WAYS

A hand-embroidered patch makes a great decoration for a shirt pocket, a tote bag, or anything else you can think of. Here, it is sewn onto a little purchased zipper wallet made of cotton canvas. In this project you can practice your embroidery skills. You will also learn how to use fusible interfacing to put the patch onto the bag.

Finished patch: approximately 4″ × 4″

THE MATERIALS

- ▷ 4 different colors of embroidery thread

- ▷ Embroidery needle

- ▷ 5″ embroidery hoop

- ▷ Square of linen (or other plain fabric) 6″ × 6″

- ▷ Disappearing-ink marker

- ▷ Square of fusible interfacing (such as Pellon Wonder-Under fusible web) 6″ × 6″

- ▷ Fabric scissors

THE STEPS

Embroidery pattern is on page 38. The stitches are described on pages 25–28.

1. Trace the pattern or draw your own embroidery design onto the fabric with a disappearing-ink marker. The design doesn't have to be exactly centered on the fabric because you will cut it out later, but make sure you have a generous border around all sides.

2. Put your fabric into the embroidery hoop. Cut a piece of embroidery thread no longer than 15″. Divide out 3 strands and thread your needle. Knot the thread.

3. Stitch the design. The pattern tells you which stitches to make in which areas.

4. When you have finished stitching, remove the fabric from the hoop. Spray a generous amount of water from the iron onto the fabric. This will make any ink that is left disappear. Press it flat by ironing it gently, right side up. Then press again, if needed.

5. Now it is time for the fusible interfacing! Cut a piece of fusible interfacing that is at least ¼″ larger all around than the design you have just embroidered.

like this!

Your finished embroidery is ready for fusible interfacing.

6. Using a hot iron, and following the fusible interfacing instructions, fuse the interfacing to the back of your embroidered design.

7. Cut out the design. You can make a square patch or any other shape as long as you leave a border (backed by the fusible interfacing) of at least ¼″ all around the design.

like this!

6.

Iron on fusible interfacing.

7.

Cut out your patch, and you're ready to fuse it on.

8. Decide where you would like to place the patch. Peel the paper off the back of the fusible interfacing. Place the patch where you want it. Use the hot iron to fuse the patch.

9. If you want to, sew around the patch with a whipstitch. This gives it a cute border and extra security.

like this!

8.

Peel off paper to fuse.

like this!

9.

Stitch a neat, pretty edge around fused-on patch.

MORE IDEAS

Have fun embroidering different patterns and combinations of stitches! The patterns for these two alternate designs are on page 38.

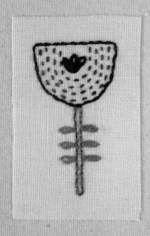

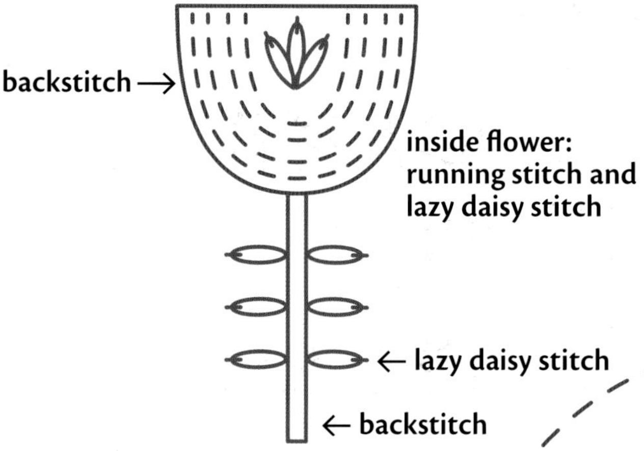

backstitch →

inside flower:
running stitch and
lazy daisy stitch

← lazy daisy stitch

← backstitch

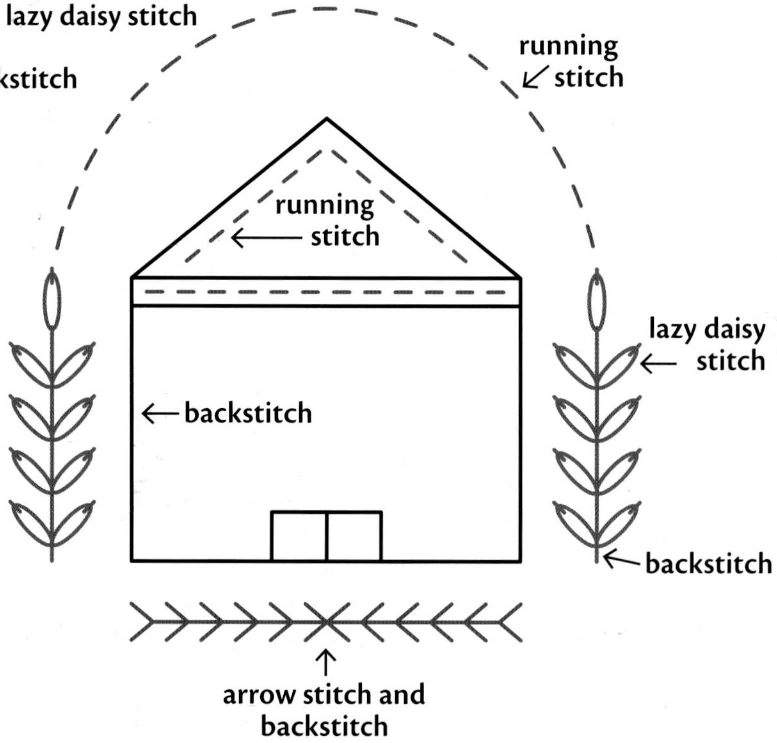

running
↙ stitch

running
← stitch

lazy daisy
← stitch

← backstitch

← backstitch

arrow stitch and
backstitch

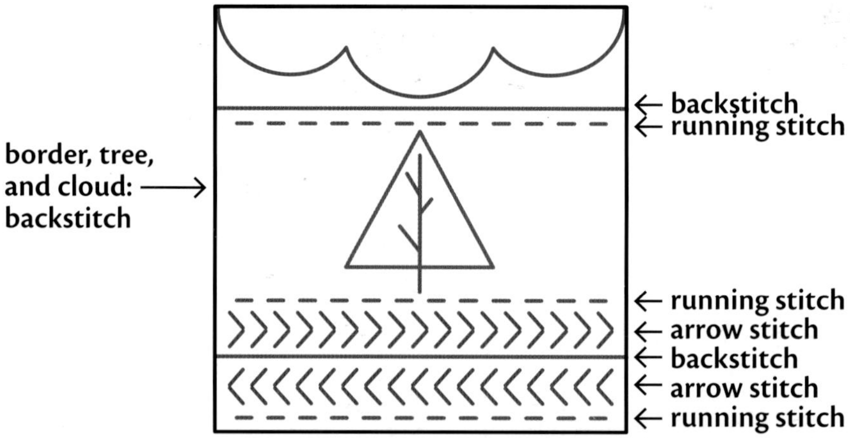

border, tree,
and cloud: →
backstitch

← backstitch
← running stitch

← running stitch
← arrow stitch
← backstitch
← arrow stitch
← running stitch

MAKE TO WEAR

Create your own style with hand-made jewelry and embroidered decorations that turn ordinary clothes into one-of-a-kind pieces. Bags, too!

COLOR WHEEL HAIR CLIPS

Let's try stitching on felt. For this project, simply stitch right over hole-reinforcement stickers to make these cute hair clips!

You can find blank hair clips at a craft store or on etsy.com. (Look for snap clips!) Hole-reinforcement stickers are easy to find in an office supply store or anyplace that sells basic school supplies.

THE MATERIALS

- ▷ Small sheet of felt (about 6″ × 6″)

- ▷ Hole-reinforcement stickers

- ▷ Embroidery thread (8″ pieces of 4 different colors for each hair clip)

- ▷ Embroidery needle

- ▷ 5″ embroidery hoop (*optional*)

- ▷ Blank hair clips

- ▷ Fabric scissors

- ▷ Hot glue gun

THE STEPS

1. Place the piece of felt in an embroidery hoop (if you're using one). Stick a few reinforcement stickers onto the felt. Leave at least ½″ between the stickers.

2. Thread a needle with all 6 strands of embroidery thread in 1 color.

3. Divide a sticker into 4 sections and use a different color of thread for each section.

Bring your needle up from the back on the outside edge of the circle. Go down again at the inside edge. Repeat with each stitch. Keep your stitches close together so that you won't see any of the sticker when you are finished. Stitch all of 1 color and *knot off*. Rethread your needle with the next color. Repeat.

like this!

1.

Put felt in hoop (*optional*) and stick hole reinforcements on it.

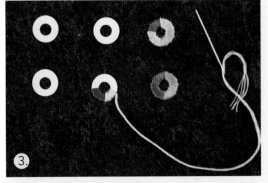

3.

Stitch around circle with 1 color of thread at a time.

COLOR WHEEL HAIR CLIPS

41

4. Stitch over all the reinforcement stickers. Take the felt out of the embroidery hoop, if you used one. Use fabric scissors to cut out the circles. Leave a small border around your stitches.

5. Attach the felt circles to blank hair clips with a hot glue gun.

Cut out circles. (Don't cut stitching!)

Glue circles on hair clips. Ready to wear or give!

MORE IDEAS

Hair clips are such great little projects to wear and give. So why not make them in a different design, too? Here's one example. Using 2 strands of embroidery thread, create a flower by completing 8 lazy daisy stitches around a central point. Use a different color of embroidery thread to fill in the petals—a small stitch in each petal will do the trick. With a third color of thread, make a circle of running stitches around the flower. Cut out the finished design, leaving a small border around the stitches, and attach to a hair clip with a hot glue gun.

▷ tip

To make a cute gift box, dress up a plain purchased one from a craft store. Just cut out a few simple shapes from colorful papers and glue them on! You can also use washi tape, as I did in the box below.

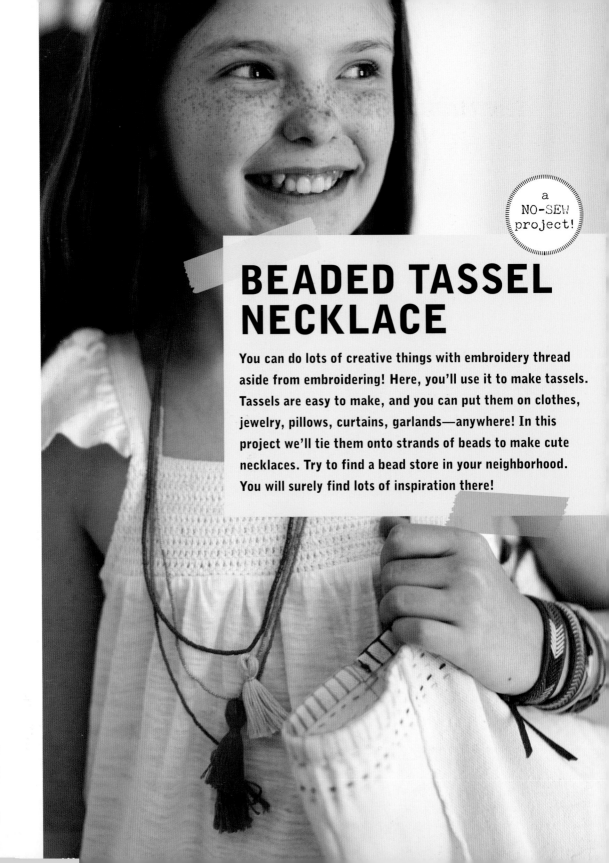

BEADED TASSEL NECKLACE

You can do lots of creative things with embroidery thread aside from embroidering! Here, you'll use it to make tassels. Tassels are easy to make, and you can put them on clothes, jewelry, pillows, curtains, garlands—anywhere! In this project we'll tie them onto strands of beads to make cute necklaces. Try to find a bead store in your neighborhood. You will surely find lots of inspiration there!

THE MATERIALS

▷ Embroidery thread (about 9′ per tassel)

▷ Piece of cardboard 2½″ × 3½″

▷ Strands of beads

▷ tip

If you want to, you can make your own selection of beads to string into a necklace instead of buying a ready-made string. You can find lots of different beads at craft stores as well as at bead stores.

THE STEPS

1. Cut off a piece of embroidery thread 12″ long and cut it in half so you have 2 pieces 6″ long. Set the pieces aside.

2. Wrap the remaining embroidery thread (all 6 strands) around the long side of the card 12 times. Carefully slide the thread off the card.

3. Tie a separate 6″ piece of thread tightly in a knot around the center of the bunch.

Wrap thread around card.

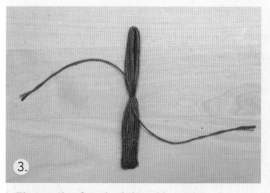

Tie together bunch of thread in center.

4. Fold the bunch of thread in half. Use another 6″ piece of thread to tie a knot around the top of the tassel.

5. With scissors, cut the tassel to the length you like.

6. Use just 1 strand of embroidery thread to tie the tassel to the strand of beads. You can hide this knot by sliding it to the inside of the tassel.

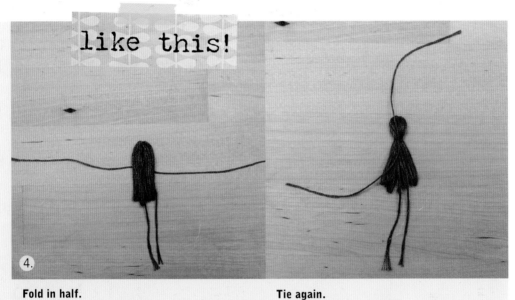

like this!

4.

Fold in half.

Tie again.

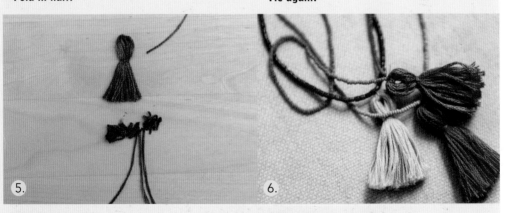

5.

Finished tassel

6.

Attach tassel to beads.

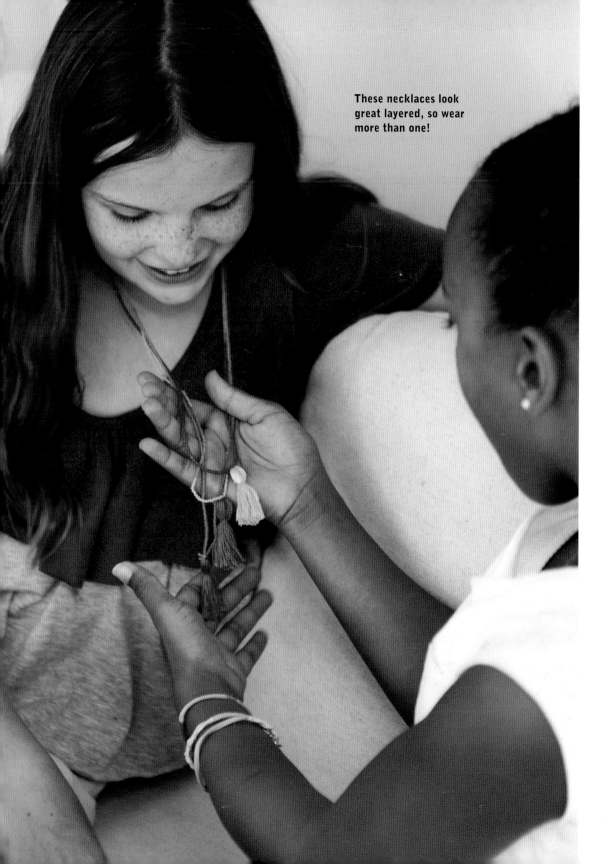

These necklaces look great layered, so wear more than one!

SIMPLY STITCHED TOTE BAG

Use some simple embroidery stitches to add a little color to a plain canvas tote bag. Look in a large craft or fabric store to find bags meant for decorating. They are also available online. You can use a white bag or a colored one. You could even add stitching to a tote that already has some kind of print or decoration on it!

THE MATERIALS

▷ Blank canvas tote bag

▷ Embroidery thread (5 or 6 different colors)

▷ Embroidery needle

THE STEPS

1. Here is your chance to use the blanket stitch (page 29)! You can do it all around the top edge of the bag. Cut a piece of embroidery thread about 15″ long. Use all 6 strands. When you start stitching, leave a tail of at least 3″.

2. Stitch a ways along the bag top. Stop stitching when you have only 3″–4″ of thread left.

3. Now change thread colors and continue with the blanket stitch. Tie the end tail of the first color of thread to the beginning tail of the next color. Continue changing colors until you have made it all the way around the bag. Then tie the final 2 tails together.

4. Below the blanket stitches, embroider 4 rows of running stitches going around the bag. Use a different color of thread for each row. Again, when you start stitching, leave a 3″ tail of thread and change colors as you did in Step 3. Finish by tying the end tail of thread to the beginning tail.

like this!

Do blanket stitch along top of bag.

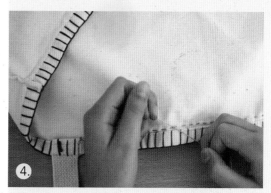

Add running stitches. Tie 2 different tails together.

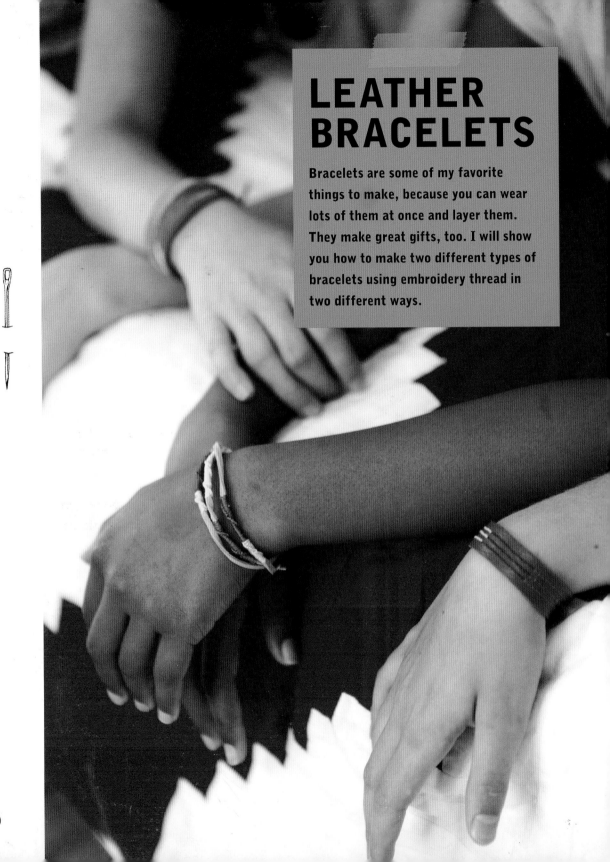

LEATHER BRACELETS

Bracelets are some of my favorite things to make, because you can wear lots of them at once and layer them. They make great gifts, too. I will show you how to make two different types of bracelets using embroidery thread in two different ways.

Easy Wrapped Bracelet

For this project, you don't even stitch with the embroidery thread. You just wrap and knot embroidery thread around leather cord. You can decide the length of the bracelet based on how many times you want it to wrap around your wrist. Look for leather cord at a craft store, in the ribbon section.

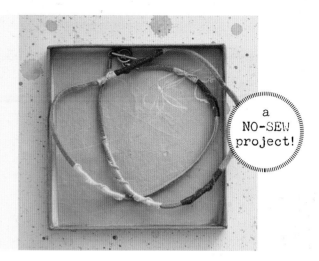

a NO-SEW project!

THE MATERIALS

- ▷ Safety pin

- ▷ Leather cord

- ▷ Embroidery thread

- ▷ Needle

- ▷ Clasp hardware (2 fold-over crimps, 2 jump rings, and a toggle clasp, from a craft store that has a jewelry-making section)

- ▷ Needle-nose pliers (small tool with pointed tips for grasping, from a hardware store or beading section of a craft store)

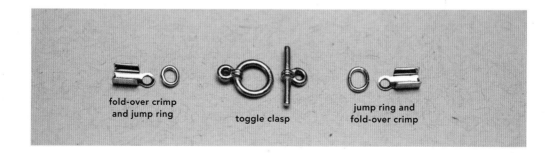

fold-over crimp and jump ring

toggle clasp

jump ring and fold-over crimp

THE STEPS

1. To figure out the bracelet length, wrap the leather cord around your wrist as many times as you like it. Cut the cord with scissors. (Remember, the clasp that you add at the end will add a little bit of length.)

2. Tie the end of the leather cord to a safety pin. Pin it to your jeans or the arm of the sofa. This will help you hold the cord taut while you wrap it.

3. For the first section of wrapping, cut a piece of embroidery thread about 18″ long. Use all 6 strands. Tie the thread in a knot around the leather cord. Leave 1 short thread tail (about 2″) and 1 long tail.

4. Wrap the long tail of the thread around the back of the cord and around the other side. Then bring it underneath itself to make another knot. Keep wrapping and knotting the thread in this way to extend the wrapped section. Wrap *over* the short tail to hide it.

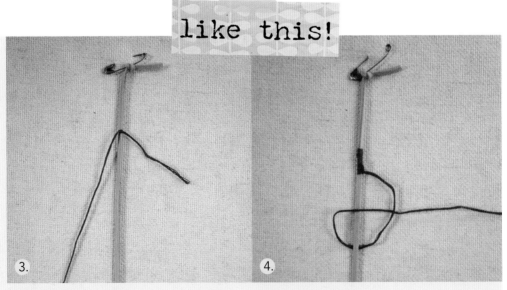

like this!

3. Knot thread on leather cord. Leave 1 short tail and 1 long tail.

4. Wrap and knot long tail.

5. When you start to run out of thread, or when you are happy with the length of the wrapped section, stop. Thread the end onto a needle. Pull the needle back up through a short section of wrapping. Snip off any extra thread that is showing.

6. Repeat Steps 3–5 several times along the length of the cord. You can decide how many wrapped sections you want and how long you want them to be. Leave some parts of the leather cord unwrapped and showing. If the new section is touching a previously wrapped section you can start it by running your needle under previous wrappings. If you want to leave a space between the wrapped sections, you'll have to start with a new knot.

7. Add the fold-over crimps, 2 jump rings, and toggle clasp. Place the end of the cord in a fold-over crimp. Use needle-nose pliers to fold down one side of the crimp and then the other. Repeat on the other end of the cord. Use a jump ring to connect the crimps to the toggle clasp.

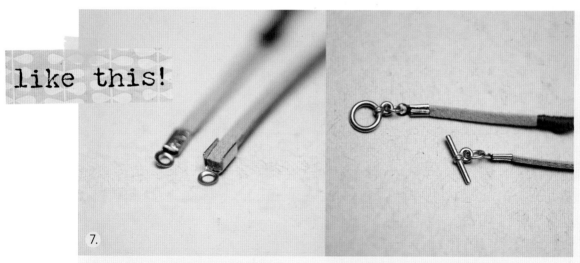

like this!

7.

Place end of cord in fold-over crimp.

Connect crimp to 1 side of clasp with jump ring.

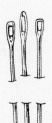

Embroidered Bracelet

Make this bracelet from recycled leather. You can find old leather purses or wallets at a thrift store and cut them apart for reuse. Leather that's worn and soft will be easiest to work with. Choose an item with a tag that says "genuine leather."

Make from recycled leather.

THE MATERIALS

- ▷ Leather strip ¼″–¾″ wide × 6″ long

- ▷ Thin leather strip about ⅛″ wide × 7″ long

- ▷ Embroidery thread in several colors

- ▷ Small needle with a narrow eye

- ▷ Sewing machine with an old needle

- ▷ Needle-nose pliers (optional, from a craft store or hardware store)

- ▷ Awl (from a craft store or hardware store)

- ▷ Scissors

▷ safety tip

You will need a tool called an awl to punch large holes in the bracelet for attaching a leather strip closure. Be very careful using this tool. The point is super sharp! Place the leather flat on a steady surface that won't be damaged by the awl point. Then push the awl through the leather.

THE STEPS

1. Cut apart a leather bag at the seams. Cut and pull away the fabric lining if there is one. You want to end up with flat pieces of leather large enough to be usable. From these pieces, measure and cut out the pieces of leather listed in The Materials.

2. You will need to prepunch holes for embroidering. Otherwise, it will be almost impossible to get your needle through the leather! Use your sewing machine to prepunch. Sew 3 rows of straight stitches with an *unthreaded* sewing machine. It is best to go slowly. I recommend using the hand wheel. Start and end the stitching at least ¼″ from each end of the strip.

3. Thread a small needle with 2 strands of embroidery thread. Stitch arrow stitches through the prepunched holes. It may be a little hard to get your needle through the holes. If so, use a small pair of pliers to grab the end of the needle and pull it through.

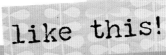

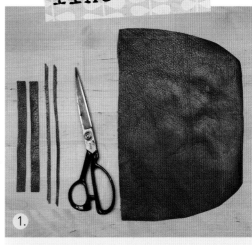

1. **Cut leather pieces.**

3. **Stitch through prepunched holes.**

4. Stitch for a short distance and *knot off the thread*. Thread the needle with the next color and continue stitching. Stitch in as many colors as you like.

5. Now for the leather strip closure. Poke the point of the awl through the leather at each end of the bracelet. Carefully push the awl through until the hole is large enough to fit the thin leather strip through it.

6. Pull the ends of the leather strip through the holes from the back side of the bracelet to the front. Put the bracelet on your wrist. Pull to tighten it, and tie. You may want to ask someone to help you tie it.

like this!

5.

Push awl point through leather. Ask adult for help!

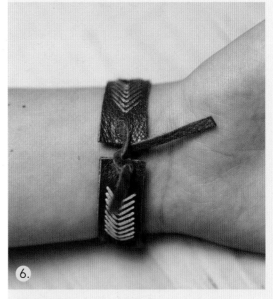

6.

Tie together leather strips to wear bracelet.

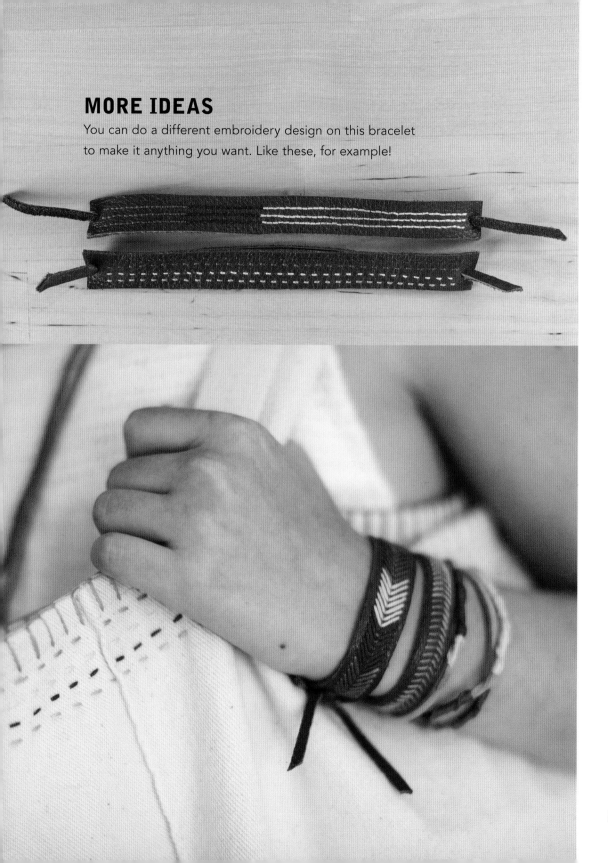

MORE IDEAS

You can do a different embroidery design on this bracelet
to make it anything you want. Like these, for example!

LOVE SHIRT

Make a plain T-shirt or tank top special with a hand-embroidered patch!

THE MATERIALS

- ▷ Plain T-shirt or tank top

- ▷ Letter patterns L, O, V, and E (see Making Letter Patterns, page 62)

- ▷ Disappearing-ink marker

- ▷ Embroidery thread (black plus 3 or 4 different colors)

- ▷ 5″ embroidery hoop

- ▷ Small piece of cotton canvas fabric (about 6″ × 8″)

- ▷ Piece of fusible interfacing (such as Pellon Wonder-Under fusible web) 5″ × 7″

- ▷ Iron

- ▷ Cardstock

- ▷ Scissors

- ▷ Computer and printer

THE STEPS

1. Follow the directions in the sidebar (page 62) to make the letter patterns. Trace around them onto the canvas fabric with a disappearing-ink marker.

Trace around letters onto canvas.

2. Put the canvas into the embroidery hoop. Using black embroidery thread, backstitch (page 26) along the outline of the letters. Then add some colorful decorative stitches to the inside of the letters. I used a whipstitch.

3. Take the canvas out of the hoop. If there is any ink showing, you can spray it with water to make it disappear. Press the canvas smooth with an iron (gently), right side up.

4. Cut a piece of fusible interfacing that is larger than the design you have just embroidered (see Step 6).

like this!

2.

Embroider outlines around letters.

Add colorful whipstitch filler.

5. Use a hot iron to fuse the interfacing to the back of the embroidered design, following the product instructions.

6. Cut out the design so the fusible interfacing completely covers the back. As shown in the photo, I cut an outline around each letter but left the letters all connected.

7. Decide where you would like to place the patch. Peel the paper off the back of the interfacing. Place the patch where you want it. Use the hot iron to fuse the patch to the shirt. Whipstitch all around the edges to make a nice fancy finish.

like this!

4.

7.

Cut fusible interfacing larger than design. Fuse to back.

Cut around design as shown.
Then iron to your shirt!

making letter patterns

To make letter patterns, you will need some cardstock and scissors. You'll also need access to a computer and printer.

1. Open a word processing application on your computer. (Use an application like Microsoft Word that you would use to write a book report.)

2. Pull down the Fonts menu from the toolbar. Choose a type font that you like. (One with a simple outline is best.) I used one called Osaka. Choose a font size. For this project, I used 168-point type.

3. Type all the letters of the alphabet that you will need for your project—in this case, L, O, V, and E. Place cardstock in your printer. Ask an adult to help you figure out how to set it up for printing.

4. Cut out the letters right on their borders. These are your patterns.

LOVE

Now you can use them to embellish a shirt—or anything else you want to dress up!

MORE IDEAS

For an alternate design you can change the types of stitches you use inside the letters. Try groups of 3 lazy daisy stitches. Keep the outline of the letters black and use a different color of thread inside each letter!

♥ SHIRT

You can use embroidered patches to make all kinds of shirt designs. This one is stitched onto Aida cloth. You can read about this cloth in Fabric (page 21). You will be able to see a clear grid in the Aida cloth that matches the grid in the pattern. This shows you where to stitch in different colors of embroidery thread to make a heart.

THE MATERIALS

▷ Plain T-shirt or tank top

▷ Piece of white Aida cloth 6″ × 6″
(I used 11-count mesh.)

▷ 5″ embroidery hoop

▷ Embroidery thread (dark green, plus
3 or 4 colors)

▷ Piece of fusible interfacing (such as
Pellon Wonder-Under fusible web)
5″ × 5″

THE STEPS

Heart embroidery pattern is on page 68.

1. Center the Aida cloth in your
embroidery hoop. Thread a needle
with 3 strands of embroidery thread.

2. First you will need to stitch the heart,
following the pattern provided. Use
as many colors as you like! Stitch the
design. The pattern shows you which
little squares on the cloth to make your
stitches in. All you have to do is count
the pattern grid squares and match
them to the Aida squares. Use whatever
colors you like, and outline the heart in
dark green.

3. When you are finished stitching,
remove the piece from the hoop. Press
gently, right side up.

Stitch the heart.

♥ SHIRT

4. Iron a piece of fusible interfacing to the back of the embroidery.

5. Cut out the heart. Leave about a ¼″ border around the stitches, making sure the fusible interfacing covers the back.

6. Peel the paper from the back of the heart. Place it where you want it to be on the shirt.

7. Use a hot iron to fuse the heart to the shirt. Do a whipstitch around the edge to finish it off.

like this!

6. Peel paper backing off cut-out heart.

7. Whipstitch around edges of fused heart.

Your new ♥ tee!

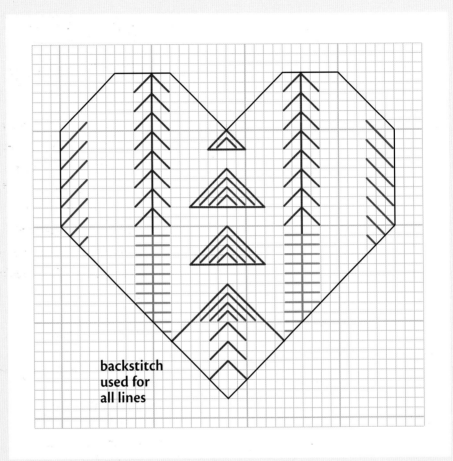

backstitch
used for
all lines

MAKE TO DECORATE

You can use your creative skills to make all sorts of beautiful projects for your room without spending much money. If you don't have your own room, you can decorate a special corner or a common area in your home. Your family will appreciate your hard work!

ARROWS WALLHANGING

It's fun to combine fabric with materials you find in nature. I live near a lake that has beaches full of smooth, interesting-shaped driftwood. I used a piece for this project. If you don't have access to driftwood, look for small fallen branches with unusual shapes. You can find them in woodsy areas or maybe even in your own backyard.

Finished wallhanging:
about 9″ × 18″

THE MATERIALS

▷ Small piece of driftwood (or a branch) in the shape of a V (9″–12″ long)

▷ Piece of wool felt 6″ × 12″

▷ 1 square 6″ × 6″ of *each* of 2 cotton printed fabrics

▷ Piece of fusible interfacing (such as Pellon Wonder-Under fusible web) 6″ × 12″

▷ Fabric scissors

▷ Embroidery thread

▷ Piece of cardstock 3″ × 3″

THE STEPS

Triangle pattern is on page 73.

1. Trace and make a triangle pattern out of cardstock.

2. Cut out 6″ × 6″ squares of 2 different fabrics and cut out 2 pieces of fusible interfacing about the same size.

3. Use a hot iron to fuse the fusible interfacing to the back side of the fabric. Don't peel off the paper yet!

4. With a pencil, trace the triangle pattern 4 or 5 times onto each piece of fused fabric. Trace on the paper side of the fusible interfacing.

Make triangle pattern.

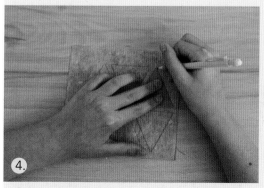

Trace triangles onto paper side of fused fabric.

5. Cut out the triangles with fabric scissors. Peel off the paper backing.

6. Fuse the triangles to the wool felt with a hot iron. Leave about ½″ between triangles.

7. Cut out the triangles again. This time leave a small ⅛″ border of felt around the triangles.

like this!

6.

Fuse triangles to wool felt with iron.

7.

Cut out fused triangles; leave 1/8″ of felt around edges.

8. Lay out the triangles in a row, alternating between the 2 fabrics. Overlap them a bit as shown. Stitch them together using embroidery thread. Starting at the point of the bottom triangle, knot all 6 strands of thread together and stitch large running stitches through the triangles' centers. Be sure to take a stitch at each triangle point as shown in the photo. Leave a long tail of thread at the top.

9. Tie the string of triangles to the center of the wood branch V. Hang up your wallhanging in a special place!

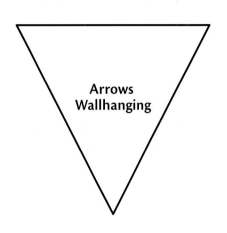

Arrows
Wallhanging

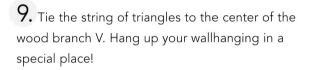

like this!

8. Stitch together overlapping triangles.

9. Tie arrows to branch and hang to display!

QUICK & EASY ORNAMENTS

Put little bits of fun printed fabric to good use! Make a collection of small ornaments to hang here, there, and everywhere. Choose a fabric that has medium- or large-sized images printed on it. You can find fabric with animals, plants, or flowers. If you use holiday-themed fabric, you could make cute Christmas tree ornaments.

THE MATERIALS

▷ Scraps of large-scale print fabrics

▷ Scraps of fusible interfacing (such as Pellon Wonder-Under fusible web)

▷ Scraps of wool felt

▷ Embroidery thread

▷ Fabric scissors

THE STEPS

1. Choose and cut out a small section of printed fabric with the image you like (the animal or flower) centered in it.

2. Cut a piece of fusible interfacing about the size of the fabric. Iron it onto the back of the printed fabric.

3. Cut out the animal or flower from the printed fabric.

Choose section of fabric with image.

Cut out around image.

4. Peel the paper off the back of the piece. Use your iron to fuse it onto a piece of wool felt a little larger than the fabric. Now cut it out again, leaving a small border of felt around the printed image.

5. Thread a needle with a small piece of embroidery thread; use 1 or 2 strands. Pull the thread through the top of the ornament. Take out the needle and tie the thread ends to make a loop for hanging.

like this!

Fuse ornament to wool and cut out, leaving border.

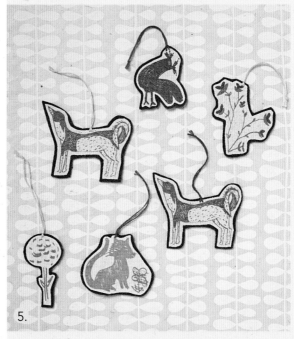

Add thread loops, and they're ready to hang!

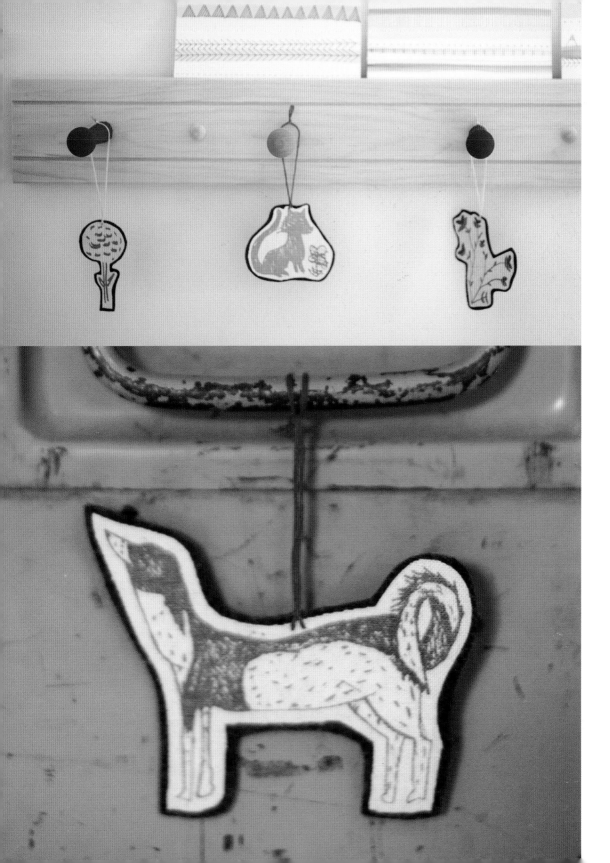

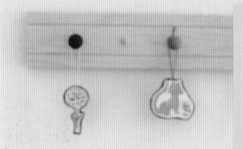

HELLO WALL ART

Make a graphic statement with an embroidered piece that sends a friendly message. Pop it into a purchased picture frame and hang it up in your favorite space. I made this framed "**HELLO**" almost the same way I made the **LOVE** Shirt (page 58). It's easy!

Finished wall art: 9″ × 11″ (includes my frame)

THE MATERIALS

▷ Picture frame (about 9″ × 11″)

▷ Fancy tape wide enough to cover the frame (if you want)

▷ Letter patterns for H, E, L, O (see Step 1, below)

▷ Piece of cotton canvas*

▷ Embroidery thread (black, plus 3 or 4 different colors)

▷ Disappearing-ink marker

▷ Embroidery hoop (size depends on cotton canvas size)

▷ Cardstock

▷ Computer and printer

The size of the canvas depends on the frame size. Measure the outside of the frame and cut a piece 1″ larger all around. For example, if your frame is 9″ × 11″, cut your fabric 11″ × 13″.

▷ **tip**

I used colorful Japanese washi tape to decorate a plain, inexpensive IKEA frame! You can find this tape (and other fun tape) online and in craft stores.

THE STEPS

1. Follow the directions in Making Letter Patterns (page 62). Make the letter patterns for H, E, L, and O. Trace around them onto the center of the canvas fabric with a disappearing-ink marker.

like this!

Trace letters onto canvas.

2. Put the canvas into the embroidery hoop. Using black embroidery thread, backstitch along the outline of the letters. Then add some colorful decorative stitches to the inside of the letters. I used a whipstitch (page 29).

3. Take the fabric out of the hoop. Press it smooth with an iron (gently), right side up.

4. Cut the fabric to the size of the frame. (Use a ruler and pencil to measure and mark it first.)

5. Smooth the canvas onto the frame's cardboard backing and secure it in the frame. Ask an adult if you need help putting it together.

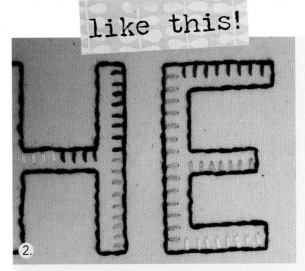

like this!

Stitch outlines around letters in black. Add colorful whipstitches as filler.

Measure, mark, and cut canvas to frame size. Hooray—now you've got wall art!

PAINTED GRAPHICS PENCIL HOLDER

If you love to make things, you will probably wind up with a lot of craft tools and supplies. You'll need to find ways to organize them! Here is an easy way to print designs on fabric and make a lovely pencil holder out of a plain old empty can.

THE MATERIALS

▷ Clean, empty food can with paper label removed

▷ Cotton canvas fabric*

▷ Scrap paper

▷ Masking tape

▷ Round color-coding labels**

▷ Fabric paint (3 colors) and brush (I used Pébéo Setacolor transparent paint and a wide flat brush.)

▷ Straight pins

▷ Embroidery thread

▷ Measuring tape

▷ Iron

* See Step 1 in The Steps to determine the size.

** Find these labels at an office supply or craft store.

THE STEPS

1. With a measuring tape, measure around the can to get the circumference. Write the circumference down and add 1″. Measure the can from top to bottom. Write the height down and add 1″. Cut a piece of cotton canvas fabric. The width should be the circumference of the can plus 1″, and the height should be the height of the can plus 1″.

2. Lay the canvas flat on the table with some scrap paper underneath.

3. Now you are going to put the masking tape and color-coding labels onto the fabric. You will paint the fabric surface that *isn't* covered by the tape and labels. Here is where you can be creative. Stick on rows of masking tape and rows of color-coding labels. Experiment with overlapping stickers and masking tape. You can have the stickers touch each other as I have done, or overlap, or leave a little space between them. Each way will give you a slightly different look.

4. Now use a paintbrush to paint the fabric that is exposed. I used 3 colors, but you can use more or fewer. (Even just 1 color would look good!)

5. Wait until the paint has completely dried. Then remove the masking tape and stickers.

6. Now it's time for the iron! You need to use the iron to heat set the fabric paint. Follow the directions on the paint container.

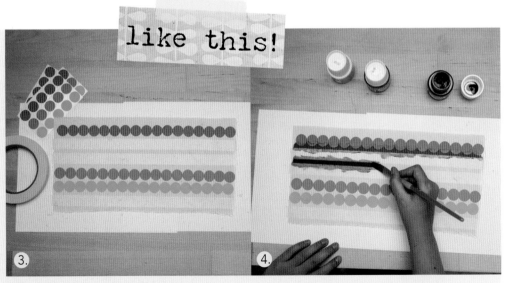

like this!

Create design with masking tape and stickers.   Paint areas around stickers and tape.

7. Iron under a hem on the edges of the fabric: Iron under ¾″ on one of the sides, and ½″ on the top and bottom.

8. The trickiest part of this project is making sure that the fabric stays tightly wrapped around the can while you stitch it closed. Wrap the fabric with the folded-under side edge going over the top of the unfolded edge. Use straight pins to hold the fabric tightly in place. You might want a helper to hold it. Sew with a whipstitch (page 29) along the side edge from the top of the can to the bottom, removing pins as you go. Then you are done!

Remove pins, and you are done!

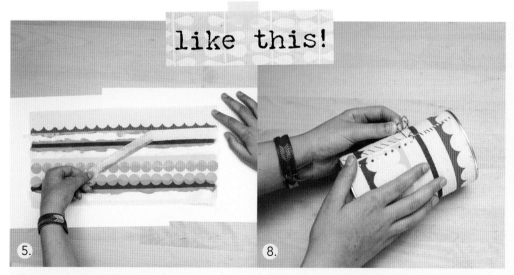

like this!

5. Remove masking tape and stickers.

8. Wrap fabric around can. Sew ends together with whipstitch, removing pins as you go.

STYLISH PILLOW COVERS

Pillows can really brighten up a room. They are fast and easy to make, too. Choose a fabric you really love, and you can't go wrong! For this project, I'll show you how to make a simple, basic pillow cover. Then you can make another one with a little extra hand-stitched pizzazz. For both, you'll need to do just a little stitching on the sewing machine. If you don't have sewing machine experience, ask an adult to help you.

Finished cover: 16″ × 16″

Basic Pillow Cover

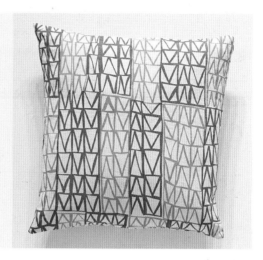

THE MATERIALS

▷ 16″ × 16″ pillow form

▷ ⅝″ yard printed fabric (min. 43″ wide)

▷ Machine sewing thread to match fabric

▷ Ruler at least 18″ long

▷ Fabric scissors

▷ Pinking shears

▷ Straight pins

▷ Iron

▷ Sewing machine

THE STEPS

1. Cut out 3 pieces of fabric. Cut 1 large piece 16½″ × 16½″ for the pillow front. Cut 2 smaller pieces, each 12″ × 16½″, for the pillow back.

▷ **tip**

Use a ruler to measure the fabric before you cut. With a pencil, mark the fabric along the ruler edges to the measurements you need for the 3 pieces. Then cut with scissors along the drawn lines.

2. On 1 long side of each back piece, turn under the edge ½″. Press it with a hot iron. Then turn the edge ½″ again to hide the raw edges. Press. Machine sew the hem in place with a straight stitch.

3. Lay the pillow front piece right side up on a flat surface. Put the 2 back pieces on top, wrong sides up. Line up the raw edges of all 3 pieces around the outside edges. The 2 back pieces will overlap in the middle. Pin the pieces together all around the edges.

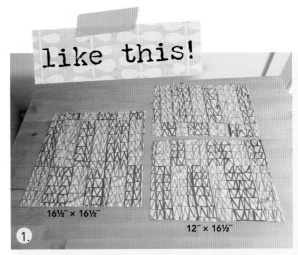

like this!

16½″ × 16½″

12″ × 16½″

1. Cut 1 piece for front and 2 pieces for back.

2. Press and machine sew ¹/₂″ hems on back pieces.

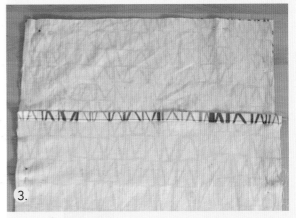

3. Layer front and back pieces. Line up edges and pin.

4. Machine sew all the way around the pillow, ½˝ from the edges. Use a straight stitch.

▷ **tip**

The distance from the edge of the fabric you are sewing to the line of stitching is usually called the <u>seam allowance</u>. Here, the seam allowance is $1/2$˝.

5. Trim the raw edges all around the pillow with pinking shears. The pinking shears will cut the fabric in a zigzag pattern. This helps keep the raw (cut) edges from fraying. Also cut across the corners. (You cut the point off but don't cut through the stitches.) This will make the corners look sharp when you turn the pillow cover right side out.

6. Turn the pillow cover right side out. Iron it smooth. Put the pillow form inside and push out the corners. The back acts like an envelope so the cover is easy to take on and off for washing!

like this!

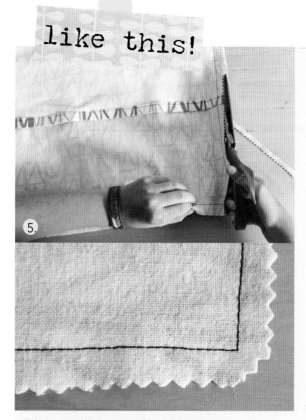

Trim seam allowance with pinking shears.

Turn right side out and admire!

Embroidered Pillow Cover

This pillow cover is made the same way as the Basic Pillow Cover, but you'll give the fabric some extra decoration before you sew it. Choose a printed fabric—one that is not super colorful. You will add color with your stitches. I used Sara Lee Parker's Grey Dogs fabric.

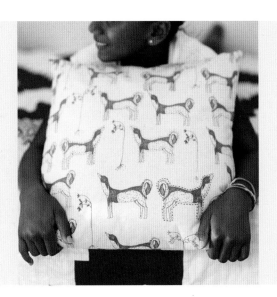

THE MATERIALS

▷ 16″ × 16″ pillow form

▷ ⅝″ yard printed fabric (min. 43″ wide)

▷ Embroidery thread in several different colors

▷ Embroidery hoop

▷ Tools used for Basic Pillow Cover (page 87)

THE STEPS

1. Cut out 3 pieces of fabric. Cut 1 large piece 16½″ × 16½″ for the pillow front. Cut 2 smaller pieces, each 12″ × 16½″, for the pillow back.

2. Put the pillow front piece in the embroidery hoop. You will probably have to do some of the embroidery and then take it out of the hoop to reposition it before stitching other parts of the fabric.

3. Use your imagination to figure out what kind of stitching to add to the fabric. If the image is a simple shape like these dogs, you can outline the shapes with a running stitch. You can also fill in some elements with stitching. Here, I used small stitches to color in a few of the leaves on the little plants.

4. When you have added all the stitching you want, take the fabric out of the hoop. Press it smooth with the right side up.

5. Follow Steps 2–6 for the Basic Pillow Cover (page 87) to make the pillow cover.

Add fun stitching.

MORE IDEAS

Here are other samples of how you might add embroidered touches to printed fabric.

FELTED DISKS GARLAND

This garland is a fun touch for any room. You can make it as long or as short as you want. You can loop it or hang it just about anywhere. For this project I felted an old wool sweater to make the soft, thick disks. I'll show you how! Depending on the sweater you use, your garland will have its own personality!

Finished sizes: disks are about 1¾″ across; garland is 4′ long

THE MATERIALS

▷ Piece of felted wool from a sweater*

▷ Embroidery thread in several colors

▷ Fabric scissors

▷ Plastic bottle or jar cap about 1¾˝ across (I used a cap from a jar of spices.)

▷ Marker

See Felting a Sweater (page 96).

THE STEPS

1. Prepare the sweater as described in Felting a Sweater (page 96). Then cut the felted sweater into the largest possible flat pieces.

2. Now you'll cut lots of small circles from the felted wool. Use a plastic bottle or jar cap to "stamp" little circles on the wool. With a marker, apply plenty of ink all around the edge of the cap. Press it down firmly onto the felt. You should see a faint circle that you can use as your guide for cutting. Repeat this to create as many circles as you want. Cut out the circles.

3. Now you'll do a blanket stitch (page 29) around the edges of the circles. Cut 24˝-long pieces of embroidery thread. Stitch halfway around a circle in 1 color of embroidery thread, using all 6 strands. Leave thread tails about 6˝ long when you start and when you

like this!

Stamp circles on felted wool with inked bottle cap.

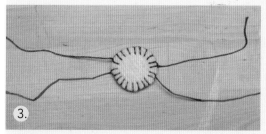

Stitch around edges using blanket stitch. Leave thread tails at beginning and end of each color thread.

FELTED DISKS GARLAND

finish. Stitch around the other half of the circle with a different color of thread. Again, leave 6″ tails when you start and finish.

4. Tie the tails together in a knot on each side of the circle. Cut 1 of the tails on each side of the circle short, and leave the others long.

5. Stitch around the rest of the circles. After you have stitched around all of them, tie the long thread ends together to make a garland.

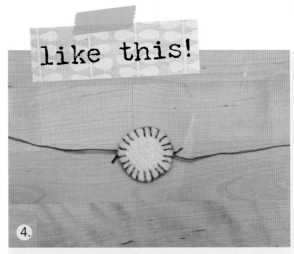

4.

Tie together tails and trim thread.

5.

Tie together and display!

Felting a Sweater

Shop in a thrift store for an old wool sweater. You can usually buy one for a few dollars. It's OK if it has a few holes! (You could also ask your parents if there are any old sweaters in the house that nobody wants anymore.)

The tag should say "100% wool."

The sweater should have a tag that says "100% wool." It should have a flat knit stitch, not a bumpy cabled or ribbed texture.

1. Put the sweater in the washing machine and set the water temperature to hot. (Ask an adult to help you if necessary.) Add laundry detergent and a squirt of dish soap. Choose a "heavy" wash cycle. Or you can run the sweater through the washing machine twice.

2. Dry the sweater in the dryer on high heat. After it comes out of the dryer, the sweater should look quite a bit smaller than it started out! You shouldn't be able to see the individual knit stitches any more. Instead, the wool will be thick, soft, and fuzzy. You can cut it up without it unraveling.

before felting

after felting

FABRIC • PAPER • THREAD

MORE FUN PROJECTS TO TRY

You can use embroidery, simple sewing, and other skills to make anything from bags to gift tags to coasters. The projects in this section show you how to do some unusual projects such as stitching on paper and using fabrics to cover things like notebooks. There are even fabric-covered magnets!

MORE FUN PROJECTS TO TRY

HEXAGON MAGNETS

These fabric-covered hexagon magnets are easy to make and fun to arrange in different ways. Put them on your fridge or any other magnetic surface. You can make beautiful designs and patterns!

You will need an adhesive magnetic sheet. You can find packages of these sheets at a craft or office supply store. They have a magnetic side and a sticky adhesive side.

A NO-SEW project!

THE MATERIALS

- ▷ 4 different pieces of solid or printed fabric 5″ × 8″ each (or slightly larger)*

- ▷ Cardstock

- ▷ Pencil

- ▷ 4 adhesive magnetic sheets 5″ × 8″*

- ▷ Scissors

* Use as many sheets and different types of fabric as you want. The more sheets, the more hexagons! You can also use a large magnetic sheet cut into smaller pieces and fabric scraps that are the same size as the pieces of magnetic sheet.

THE STEPS

Hexagon pattern is on page 100.

1. Photocopy the hexagon pattern and cut it out. Trace around it onto cardstock and cut it out.

2. Peel the paper off the sticky sides of the magnetic sheets. Press down the fabric pieces to cover the sheets. Make sure to cover the entire magnetic sheet with fabric. If you have a little extra fabric hanging off, that's OK.

like this!

2.

Stick fabrics to sticky side of magnetic sheet.

3. With a pencil, trace the hexagon shape onto the magnetic side of the sheet. Trace as many hexagons as will fit. You can fit 10–12 shapes on a 5″ × 8″ sheet, depending on the orientation of the hexagons.

4. Cut out the hexagons. Cut on the lines as carefully as you can, so that your finished hexagons will fit together nicely.

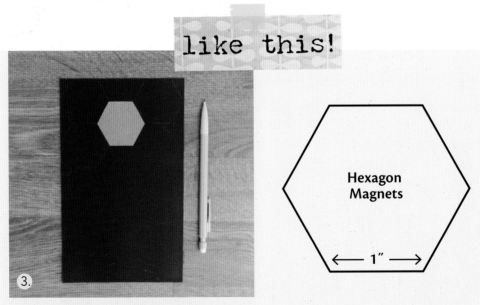

like this!

3.

Trace hexagons onto magnetic sheet.

Hexagon
Magnets

← 1″ →

Now you can arrange and rearrange your hexagons on any other magnetic surface!

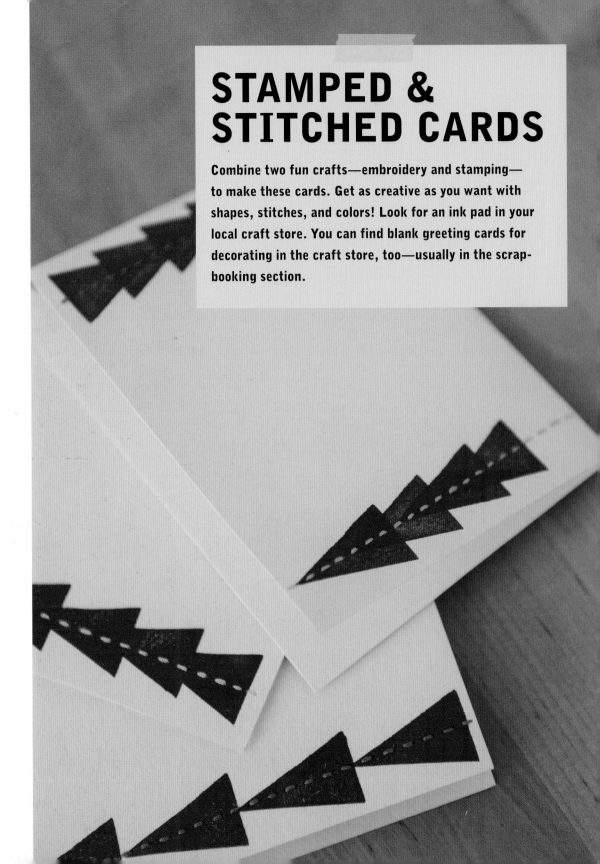

STAMPED & STITCHED CARDS

Combine two fun crafts—embroidery and stamping—to make these cards. Get as creative as you want with shapes, stitches, and colors! Look for an ink pad in your local craft store. You can find blank greeting cards for decorating in the craft store, too—usually in the scrapbooking section.

THE MATERIALS

▷ Rectangular rubber eraser

▷ Kitchen knife and cutting board

▷ Ink pad in your favorite color

▷ Blank cards

▷ Thumbtack

▷ Cardboard (a piece bigger than the blank card)

▷ Embroidery thread and needle

THE STEPS

1. Follow the steps in Simple Stamping (page 105) to make a stamp and decorate your card. I made a triangle stamp.

2. You can stitch outlines around the triangles or stitch on top of them. It's up to you! Place the card on top of a piece of cardboard, on the cutting board. Punch holes for the stitches using a thumbtack. Make holes where you will want the needle to come up and go back down. Try to space the holes evenly.

3. Thread a needle with embroidery thread. I used 3 strands of embroidery thread. You can use a simple running stitch to outline the triangles or stitch through them.

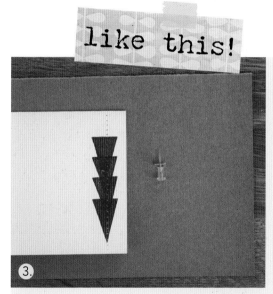

Poke holes in the card with a thumbtack and then outline designs using running stitch.

4. When you are finished stitching, you can tie the tails together in a small knot on the back. Or just cut them short and glue them down to the back of the paper.

Cut tails short and glue them down to the back of the paper.

Ready for sending!

Simple Stamping

You will need a kitchen knife to cut the rubber eraser to make a stamp. Ask an adult in your house which knife is OK to use. Be very careful when you are cutting! You don't want the knife to slip and cut your fingers! Work on a sturdy cutting board.

1. Use a pencil to draw a triangle shape on the rubber eraser. With a knife, carefully cut out the shape. This is going to be your stamp. Gently rub off any crumbs of rubber.

2. Practice stamping on a piece of scrap paper before stamping the card. Ink up the eraser stamp. Make sure the whole stamping surface is covered, but don't get it *too* wet. Press the stamp down firmly on the paper. Don't wiggle it around! Lift it straight off the paper. Practice until you get comfortable with it.

3. Plan where to place the triangle shapes on the blank card. Ink up the stamp and carefully stamp the card.

4. Let the ink dry completely.

FABRIC-COVERED NOTEPAD

Do you need a notepad to keep track of to-do lists? Or do you like writing little notes to friends? You can make a beautiful fabric cover to fit any notepad. If you want to make an embroidered cover, see More Ideas (page 109).

Finished notepad: 4″ × 6″

A NO-SEW project!

THE MATERIALS

- ▷ Notepad (4″ × 6″), from an office supply or stationery store

- ▷ 2 pieces of cardboard 4½″ × 6½″

- ▷ 2 pieces of colored cardstock 4¼″ × 6¼″

- ▷ 1 piece of colored cardstock 5½″ × 6½″

- ▷ 1 piece of pretty printed fabric 5½″ × 14½″

- ▷ Glue

- ▷ Old brush for glue

▷ **tip**

The best kind of cardboard to use for this project is the type that would be the last page of a sketchbook or notebook. I always save those pieces when I have them.

THE STEPS

1. Lay the fabric on your worktable with the wrong side up. (Put some scrap paper under the fabric to keep glue off the table.) Brush the backs of the 4½″ × 6½″ cardboard pieces with glue. (Cover the whole cardboard surface with a thin, even layer of glue.) Carefully place the cardboard pieces on the fabric. Leave ½″ spaces around the cardboard and between the 2 pieces of cardboard.

like this!

1.

Lay glued cardboard pieces on fabric, leaving ¹/₂″ space all around.

2. Brush glue around 3 of the exposed edges of each of the cardboard pieces from Step 1. (Don't spread glue along the 2 sides that are ½″ apart.) Fold the fabric over the edges. Press with your fingers until the fabric stays in place.

3. Now you are going to hide the cardboard and the fabric edges with colored cardstock. Brush the backs of the 4¼″ × 6¼″ pieces of colored cardstock with glue. Center the cardstock pieces over the cardboard pieces and then slide the cardstock pieces over a little to cover the cardboard edges near the middle of the fabric. Press them into place.

4. Use the last piece of colored cardstock to make a pocket to slide the back of the notepad into. Cut the bottom 2 corners of the cardstock as shown in the photo. Fold the bottom and sides up ½″. Carefully glue only the folded part. Fold the glued edges under. Finger-press the pocket into place on the bottom side of the notepad. Place a book or something heavy on it until it is dry.

like this!

2.

Glue and fold edges down.

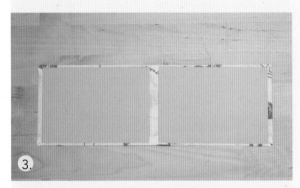

3.

Glue on colored cardstock to hide edges.

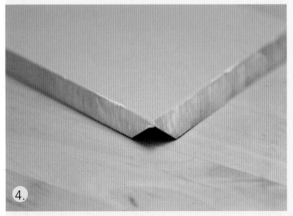

4.

Glue folded edges and then stick to notepad.

5. After the glue has dried, slide the cardboard back of the 4″ × 6″ notepad into the pocket.

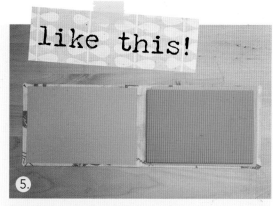

like this!

⑤

Insert back of notepad into pocket.

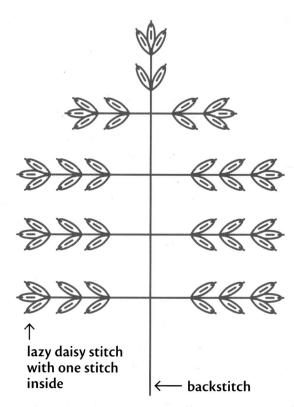

↑
lazy daisy stitch
with one stitch
inside

← backstitch

MORE IDEAS

You can embroider a fabric cover for a notepad that makes it extra special. Use the pattern (above) to stitch a design before gluing.

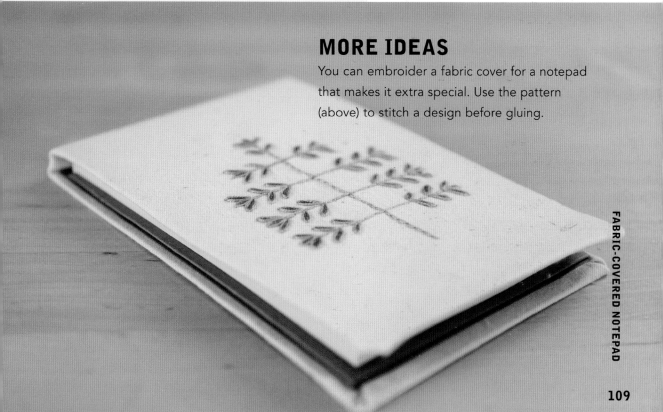

A NO-SEW project!

SKETCHBOOK
WITH POM-POM BOOKMARK

Bright, fluffy yarn pom-poms are a great no-sew project. They are so easy to make, and you can dangle them everywhere—from your backpack to your bedposts. Here, I'll show you how to make a cute bookmark that has three pom-poms. It attaches to a sketchbook.

THE MATERIALS

- ▷ Yarn (3 colors, about 6 yards of each)

- ▷ Piece of cardboard about 2½″ × 4″

- ▷ 1 sheet of fancy paper (Look in the craft store scrapbooking section.)

- ▷ Sketchbook (that you want to add the bookmark to)

- ▷ Scrap paper

- ▷ Glue

- ▷ Glue brush

- ▷ Paper scissors

THE STEPS

1. Cut a piece of yarn about 18″ long. Put it aside. Make your first pom-pom by wrapping the remaining yarn around the piece of cardboard 30–35 times.

2. Carefully slide the yarn off the cardboard. Use the piece of yarn from Step 1 to tie the bunch of yarn in the middle. When you tie, make sure you end up with 1 short tail and 1 long tail.

like this!

1. Wrap yarn around cardboard.

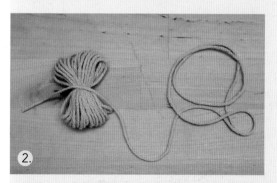

2. Slide yarn off cardboard and tie.

3. Now start trimming the bunch of yarn into a ball shape. Trim little by little until you have a pom-pom the size you want. Make sure you don't trim the long tail. You will need it!

4. Repeat Steps 1–3 twice more with the other yarn to make a total of 3 pom-poms. Braid the 3 long tails together. This is the bookmark!

5. Now make the pom-pom bookmark a permanent part of your sketchbook. Open the front cover of the sketchbook. Lay it down opened onto a piece of fancy paper. Use a pencil to trace all around the book with the cover open. The paper will cover the inside cover and the first page of the book.

6. Cut out the paper along the line that you traced.

like this!

3.

Trim yarn into pom-pom shape.

4.

Braid pom-pom tails to make bookmark.

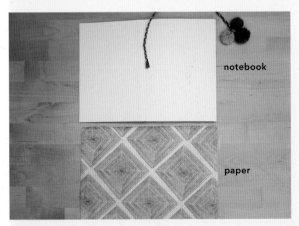

notebook

paper

Cut paper to fit inside of book.

7. Brush the back of the paper all over with glue. (Use the scrap paper to protect your table.) Place the bookmark in the sketchbook with the pom-poms above the book. A section of the braided end should be right in the crease of the inside front cover. Carefully glue the paper inside the front cover. The decorative paper will hold the bookmark in place. (Make sure the remaining length of the bookmark is just a little longer than the height of the book.)

like this!

7.

Place bookmark in crease and glue down paper.

If you want to, you can cut out a few small shapes of colorful scrap paper and glue them to the front of the book. Now it's truly custom-made!

STITCHED NOTEBOOK

A plain notebook looks special when you do a little simple stitching on the front cover. These notebooks make great little gifts for friends. You can stitch a design like the one shown in the project photo or make up your own design. You can even personalize the notebook by stitching your initials (or your friend's).

THE MATERIALS

▷ Notebook with plain cardstock cover (I used a Moleskine Cahier Pocket Ruled Notebook, 3½″ × 5½″, which comes in a pack of 3. You can also find inexpensive plain-cardstock-cover notebooks at muji.us/store/stationery/notebooks.)

▷ Pencil

▷ Thumbtack

▷ Embroidery thread (1 or several colors)

▷ Cardboard (larger than the notebook cover)

▷ Glue (*optional*)

THE STEPS

1. Draw your design lightly on the notebook cover with a pencil.

2. Place a piece of cardboard between the cover and the first page of the notebook. With a thumbtack, prepunch holes for stitching. Make holes where you will want the needle to come up and go back down. Try to space them evenly.

1. Draw cover design in pencil.

2. Punch holes with thumbtack.

3. Thread a needle with 3 strands of embroidery thread. Stitch over the pencil lines.

4. When you are finished stitching, you can tie the tails together in a small knot on the back or just cut them short and glue them down to the back of the cover.

▷ **tip**

If you want to cover up the stitching on the inside cover, you could cut out a piece of colorful paper the size of the cover. Then just glue it on the inside cover after the stitching is complete.

5. Carefully erase any pencil lines that you can still see after you have finished stitching.

like this!

4.

Tie off and cut thread tails on back so they look neat.

Finished notebook to use or give

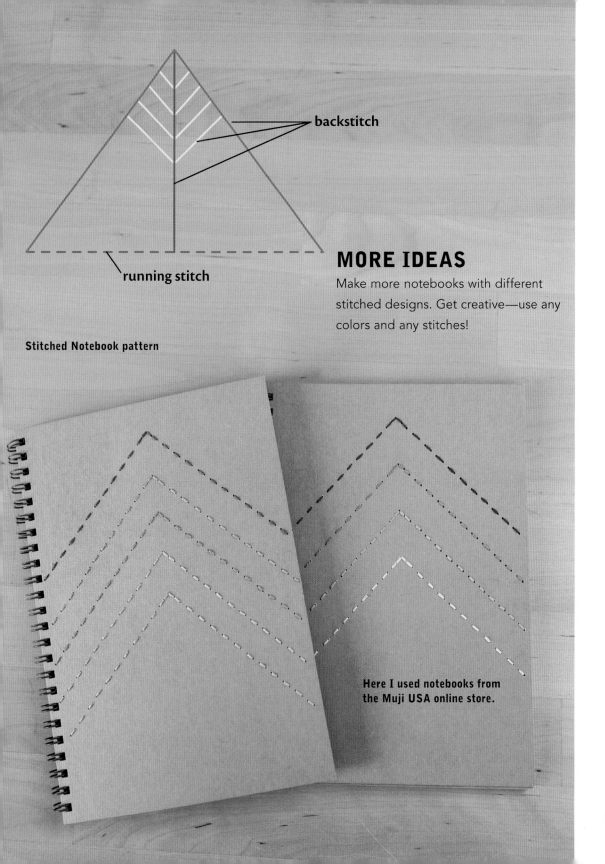

backstitch

running stitch

Stitched Notebook pattern

MORE IDEAS

Make more notebooks with different stitched designs. Get creative—use any colors and any stitches!

Here I used notebooks from the Muji USA online store.

FELTED DISK COASTERS

These fun fuzzy coasters are great to use with a glass or cup on your desk or by the TV. They are made in the same way as the Felted Disks Garland (page 92), except that they are bigger circles. Make one or make a bunch!

Finished coaster: about 3″ across

THE MATERIALS

▷ Piece of felted wool from a sweater

▷ Embroidery thread in several colors

▷ Round jar lid about 3″ across

▷ Fabric scissors

▷ Marker

▷ **tip**
Look at Felting a Sweater (page 96) to learn how to turn an old sweater into soft, thick "fabric" for these coasters.

THE STEPS

1. Prepare the sweater as described in Felting a Sweater. Then cut the felted sweater into the largest possible flat pieces.

2. The jar lid will be your "pattern" for the coasters. With a marker, apply plenty of ink all around the edge of the lid. Press it down firmly onto the felted wool. You should see a faint circle that you can use as your guide for cutting. Repeat this to make as many circles as you want. Cut out the circles.

like this!

Mark circles on felted wool with inked jar lid.

3. Blanket stitch (page 29) around the edges of the circles. You can use 1 color all the way around, or you can change thread colors once or twice. When you change colors, tie the end tail of one color to the beginning tail of the next color.

4. You can cut the tails short or you can "bury" them inside the felt. That way, you won't be able to see them at all! Thread a tail onto your embroidery needle. Pass the needle right into the middle of the layers of felt for about 1½˝ and then out again. Cut off the embroidery thread right at the point where it comes out of the felt. You can hide all the tails in this way.

like this!

3.

Stitch around edges using blanket stitch. Tie together thread tails.

4.

Bury thread tails inside felted wool to hide them.

HOLD-ANYTHING DRAWSTRING BAG

This simple sewing project is great for using up smaller pieces of fabric. You can make the bags in any size and use them to store small odds and ends, or use them to wrap gifts. If you make the bag the size shown here, the Fabric-Covered Notepad (page 106) will fit into it perfectly!

Finished size: 6″ × 7¾″

THE MATERIALS

- ▷ 1 piece of fabric 7″ × 18″
- ▷ 2 pieces of string, each 22″ long
- ▷ Machine sewing thread
- ▷ Sewing machine
- ▷ Pinking shears
- ▷ Iron

THE STEPS

1. On each short end of the fabric piece, press under ¼″ of fabric. Machine sew in place with a straight stitch.

2. Fold the fabric in half with the right sides together (wrong sides facing out).

3. Sew down 1 side of the bag, starting 2″ down from the top. Do the same thing on the other side. Sew the seams ½″ from the edges of the fabric (a ½″ seam allowance).

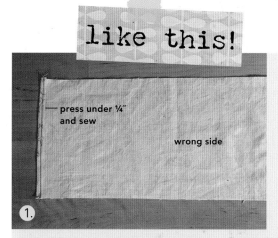

Press ends under ¹/₄″ and sew.

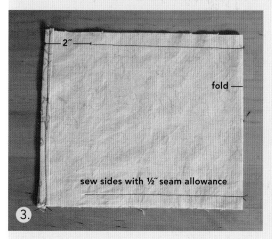

Sew bag side seams.

4. Use pinking shears to trim the raw (cut) edges on the sides. This helps keep them from fraying.

5. Use a hot iron to press the side seams open. Sew around the opening on the top, pivoting just past where the seam starts.

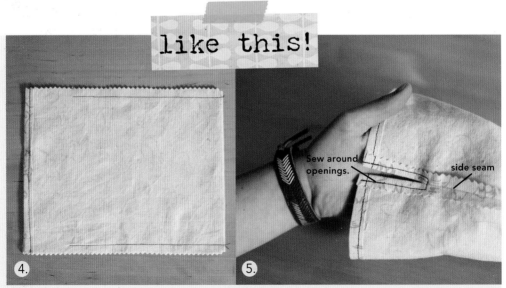

like this!

4. Trim edges with pinking shears.

5. Press side seams open and sew around openings.

Sew around openings.

side seam

6. Fold the top of the bag down 1˝ on the wrong side. Sew all the way around the bag a little less than 1˝ from the top. (Don't sew the front to the back of the bag!) This makes a channel for the drawstrings. Turn the bag right side out. Press it smooth.

7. Now for the drawstrings. The first piece of string will go in the *left* side of the bag and come back out the *left* side. The other string will start and end on the *right* side. To run the strings through the channel, tie one end of the first string to a safety pin. Then scoot the safety pin through the channel with your fingers. Repeat with the second string.

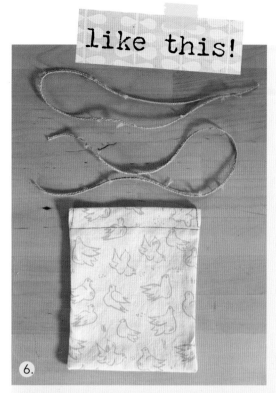

6.

Fold and sew channel around top for drawstrings; turn right side out.

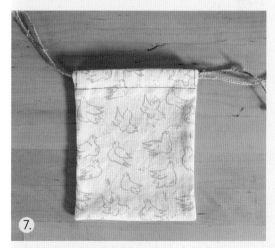

7.

Feed string through channels.

8. On each side, tie the 2 tails together into a knot. Pull the strings outward. Your bag will cinch up and close!

like this!

Tie string tails into knot on each side.   Pull to close bag.

STITCHED PAPER GIFT TAGS

Simple wrapping paper looks great with a handmade gift tag. All you need to make these gift tags is some heavy cardstock and embroidery thread. Why not make a bunch? Then you will always have some ready for gift giving.

THE MATERIALS

▷ Cardstock or heavy handmade paper

▷ Scissors or paper cutter

▷ Needle

▷ Embroidery thread (1 or 2 colors per tag)

▷ Thumbtack

THE STEPS

Embroidery patterns are on pages 130 and 131.

1. Cut the cardstock into 2″ × 3″ rectangles.

2. Use a pencil to trace or sketch your design lightly onto each gift tag. You can copy the designs on the embroidery patterns, or, of course, you can make up your own! I planned my designs so that the stitching would start and end at the top middle of the tag.

3. Place a piece of cardboard under the tag. With a thumbtack, punch small holes for stitching. Punch holes where you will want the needle to come up and go back down. Try to space them evenly.

4. After you have punched all the holes, erase the pencil lines.

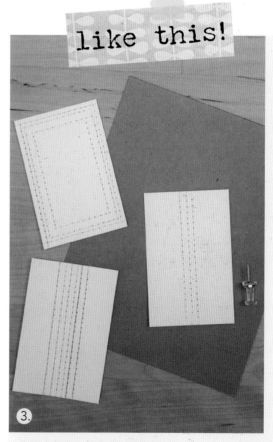

like this!

Punch holes with thumbtack.

5. Cut a piece of embroidery thread about 2′ long. You can use all 1 color for a tag, or you can stitch some rows in 1 color and some in another. For this project I used 3 strands of thread. Thread your needle.

6. Now it's time to stitch. Start your stitches at the top of the gift tag, leaving about a 4″ tail. Stitch through the holes. End at the top of the gift tag near where you started. Leave another 4″ tail at the end.

7. Tie the 2 tails together in a knot. Leave the tails on so you can attach the tag to the gift.

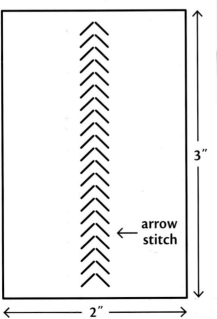

arrow stitch

3″

2″

like this!

Stitch through holes to create design. Start and end stitches at middle of top edge of tag.

Tie thread tails.

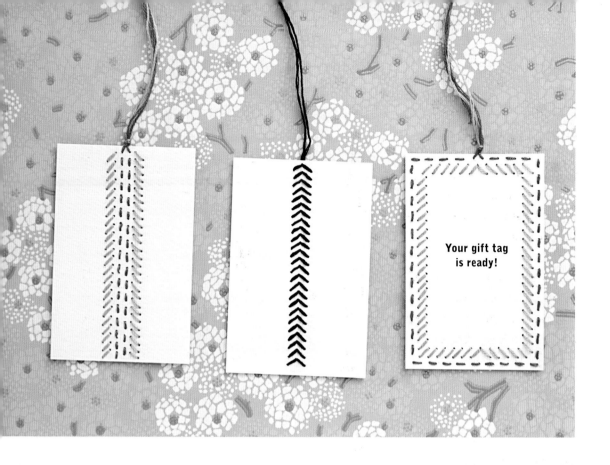

Your gift tag
is ready!

Stitched Paper Gift Tags patterns

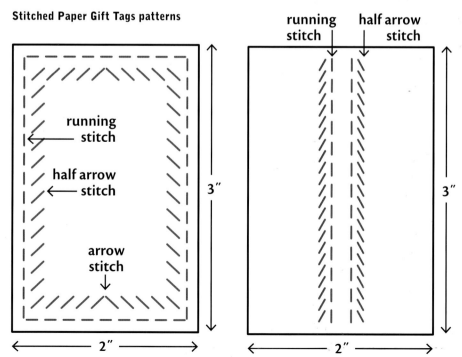

running
stitch

half arrow
stitch

running
stitch

half arrow
stitch

arrow
stitch

3"

2"

3"

2"

CROSS-STITCHED BACKPACK LABEL

This is a counted cross-stitch project. The basic stitch is in the shape of an x. All the small x's together make up the design. You can refer to Embroidery (page 26) to learn how to do the basic cross-stitch.

You will have to count the number of x's in the pattern to reproduce the image on plastic canvas. Think of every 4 holes in the canvas (2 across and 2 down) as a square in the pattern grid.

Finished label: 8½″ × 5¼″

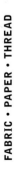

THE MATERIALS

▷ 1 plastic cross-stitch canvas sheet 8½″ × 11″, 14-mesh (I used Darice 14-mesh perforated plastic canvas sheets.)

▷ Embroidery thread in 7 different colors

▷ Embroidery needle

▷ Scissors

THE STEPS

Cross-stitch pattern is on page 135.

1. For this project I used 2 strands of embroidery thread for the cross-stitching. For each color, cut a piece of thread about 15″ long and divide out 2 strands. If you end up needing more thread, just start another piece.

2. Stitch the design according to the pattern. Each pattern grid square equals 1 cross-stitch. The piece of plastic canvas is larger than you need for the backpack label. Just make sure to work near the center of the sheet. You can cut out the patch when you are finished.

3. When you have finished stitching, carefully cut out the design. Leave an extra row of holes going all the way around. You will stitch through these to attach the label to your backpack.

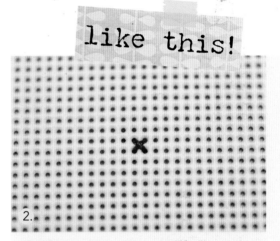

like this!

Make cross-stitch in each square.

Work near center of plastic canvas.

CROSS-STITCHED BACKPACK LABEL

4. Open your backpack. Carefully safety pin the label on the front where you want it. It will be easiest to put it near the top or on a pocket flap. Do a running stitch around the edges of the canvas and through the backpack. Leave a thread tail on the inside at the beginning of your stitching. Work slowly and check the front often to make sure the label is straight. This can be tricky, so ask an adult if you need help. When you come back to the beginning, leave another thread tail on the inside. Tie the 2 tails together to finish.

like this!

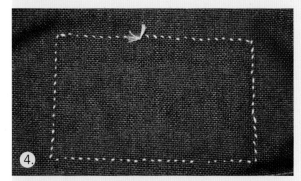

Cut out finished design. Leave extra row of holes all around.

Stitch label to backpack. Stitches go through front and into inside of backpack.

Running stitches make a neat frame on outside. Grab and go!

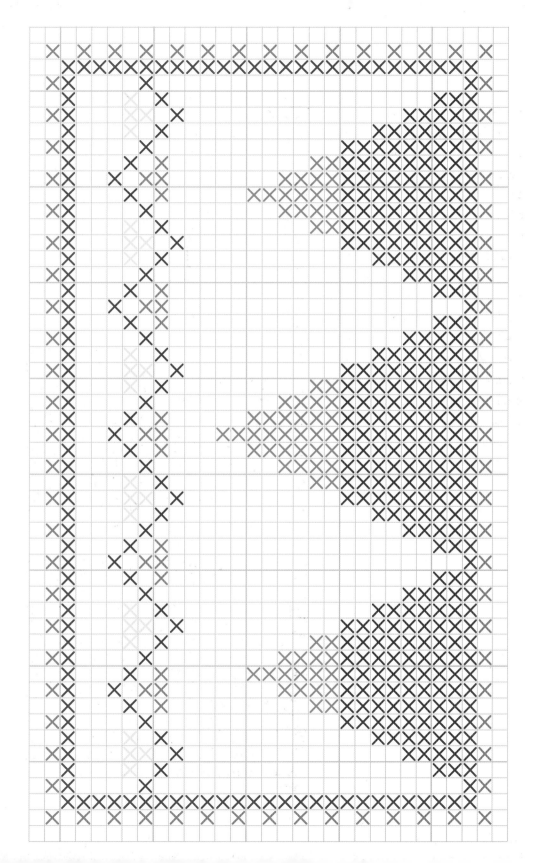

Crafting Terms to Know

AIDA CLOTH

Aida cloth is a special fabric that is usually used for cross-stitching. Because of the way it is woven, you can see tiny squares in the fabric, and each square can be occupied by one cross-stitched x.

ARROW STITCH

Arrow stitch is a type of hand embroidery stitch. Two small stitches come together to form a point that resembles an arrowhead. (Sometimes this is also called arrowhead stitch.)

AWL

An awl is a long pointed tool used for piercing holes in leather.

BACKSTITCH

Backstitch is a type of hand embroidery stitch. It is useful for stitching straight or curvy lines, and it looks like a continuous line of stitching.

BLANKET STITCH

Blanket stitch is a hand sewing stitch used to reinforce the edge of a fabric. It is more decorative than a simple whipstitch.

CANVAS

Canvas is a heavy-duty woven fabric. You can find inexpensive cotton canvas in the utility fabric section of a fabric store.

CARDSTOCK

Cardstock is a kind of paper that is thicker and stronger than regular printing paper but still flexible. (Think of the paper used for greeting cards or invitations.)

COUNTED CROSS-STITCH

Counted cross-stitch is a type of embroidery in which x-shaped stitches are used together to create a picture. A graph paper pattern is often followed to create the picture, or sometimes the pattern is printed directly onto the fabric.

CROSS-STITCH

Cross-stitch is a type of hand embroidery in which two small stitches overlap each other to form an x. Many x's stitched together can create a picture.

DISAPPEARING-INK MARKER

A disappearing-ink marker is a type of pen used for marking fabric. You can use it to draw or trace embroidery designs. When you are finished stitching you can erase the ink with just a little bit of water. Some of these markers are also made with ink that simply disappears over time, and they are called air-erasable pens. The heat of an iron can make some ink become permanent, so test your marker out before using it on your project.

EMBROIDERY HOOP

An embroidery hoop is used to hold fabric taut while you embroider. The most common type is made of two circles and can be tightened or loosened to accommodate different types of fabric.

EMBROIDERY NEEDLE

An embroidery needle is a sewing needle with a larger, elongated eye to make it easier to thread thicker threads or multiple strands for embroidery.

EMBROIDERY SAMPLER

An embroidery sampler is a piece of needlework used to demonstrate and practice different types of embroidery stitches.

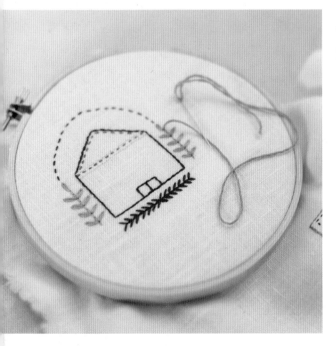

EMBROIDERY THREAD (OR FLOSS)

You can do embroidery with different types of thread or yarn, but the most common (and the type I used for the projects in this book) is 100% cotton embroidery thread. It is widely available in craft supply stores and is made up of six strands that can be easily separated from each other. The brand I use is DMC.

FELT

Felt is a type of matted fabric. It is not woven, so the edges won't fray when you cut it. Craft felt is inexpensive and is made from plastic fibers. Felt can also be made from natural fibers such as wool.

FELTING

Felting is the process of transforming old knitted wool material into felt by washing it in the washing machine. The hot water, soap, and agitation of the washing machine cause the wool fibers to bond together and form a matted material. (There are other ways to felt wool, but this is the process that I talk about in this book.)

FUSIBLE WEB OR FUSIBLE INTERFACING

Fusible web or fusible interfacing is a type of iron-on adhesive for fabric. It can be used to stiffen a fabric or to bond two fabrics together. For the projects in this book I use a paper-backed interfacing called Pellon 805 Wonder-Under fusible web.

HOT GLUE GUN

A hot glue gun is an electric tool used for melting and applying hot glue. Hot glue is sticky when it is melted and hot, and it hardens when it cools.

LAZY DAISY STITCH

Lazy daisy stitch is a type of hand embroidery stitch that resembles a petal of a flower or a small leaf.

LINEN

Linen is a type of woven fabric made from the fibers of flax plants. Flax doesn't require pesticides to grow, so it is naturally organic.

NEEDLE-NOSE PLIERS

Needle-nose pliers are a small tool with pointed tips for grasping objects.

PINKING SHEARS

Pinking shears are a type of scissor that cuts fabric in a zigzag pattern to prevent it from fraying.

PERFORATED PLASTIC CANVAS

Perforated plastic canvas is a flexible vinyl sheet with small holes in it. It is useful for some embroidery projects because it is sturdy and won't warp or fray.

POM-POM

A pom-pom is a fluffy ball of yarn, like you would find on the top of a winter hat.

RUNNING STITCH

Running stitch is a type of hand embroidery stitch. It is the most basic and simple stitch, and it is created by bringing the needle up and down through the fabric in a line.

SEAM ALLOWANCE

Seam allowance is the distance between the stitching and the raw edge of the fabric. A typical seam allowance is about ½˝.

TASSEL

A tassel is a bunch of thread or yarn that is tied together on one end. It is used as a decoration on clothing and other textile items.

TRANSFER PAPER

Transfer paper can be used to transfer an embroidery pattern from paper onto fabric. The paper is coated on one side with a type of ink that will transfer onto fabric but wash out easily when you are finished stitching. You will need to use a dark-colored transfer paper for light-colored fabrics and white transfer paper for dark-colored fabrics.

WASHI TAPE

Washi tape is a kind of masking tape that is made in Japan. It comes in many colors and patterns, so it is fun to use for craft projects or decorating cards, frames, gift boxes, and so on. You can buy it online at cutetape.com.

WHIPSTITCH

Whipstitch is a hand sewing stitch used to finish or reinforce the edge of a fabric.

About the Author

Kristen has been a maker for as long as she can remember. Her grandmother taught her how to cross-stitch when she was very young. Kristen studied ceramics in college but gravitated back to the softer side of crafting when her daughter was born. She lived in Japan for three years; there she fell deeply in love with fabric and craft books. She loves nothing more than to cuddle up on the sofa in the evenings with a needle and thread. She lives in Oberlin, Ohio, with her husband and daughter.

Kristen blogs at newhouseproject.com.